AFTER MANY YEARS

AFTER MANY YEARS

A TALE

OF EXPERIENCES & IMPRESSIONS
GATHERED IN THE COURSE
OF AN
OBSCURE LIFE

by

W E HEITLAND

MA

'Reaching forth unto those things which are before.'
Phil 3 § 13

CAMBRIDGE
AT THE UNIVERSITY PRESS
1926

CAMBRIDGE
UNIVERSITY PRESS

University Printing House, Cambridge CB2 8BS, United Kingdom

Published in the United States of America by Cambridge University Press, New York

Cambridge University Press is part of the University of Cambridge.

It furthers the University's mission by disseminating knowledge in the pursuit of education, learning and research at the highest international levels of excellence.

www.cambridge.org
Information on this title: www.cambridge.org/9781107626102

© Cambridge University Press 1926

First published 1926
First paperback edition 2013

A catalogue record for this publication is available from the British Library

ISBN 978-1-107-62610-2 Paperback

PREFACE

IT has become an ordinary thing for men who have lived beyond the traditional span of life to set down on paper a record of their experiences and to note the changes that have come under their observation in the course of time. In the case of those whose lot it has been to bear a part in great public movements, or to fill a distinguished place in some profession of general interest, their recollections find many readers. The same may be said of numerous records of travel and adventure. I have no such claim to a hearing, for I can only speak of small events in a narrow sphere of experience. From childhood to old age circumstances have gripped me fast. The ambitions of a professional career, the longing to go round the world, have been dreams now vanished for ever. Yet in my humble course I have seen changes in several parts of the country so striking and significant that I venture to record them in the form of narrative, keeping mere personal details as far as possible in the background. Narrative carries with it a certain amount of criticism. I have striven hard to observe truth in the one and fairness in the other.

Happy are those whose theme is redeemed by circumstances from the reproach of flat triviality. When Dorothy Wordsworth (14 May 1802) records 'William tired himself with seeking an epithet for the cuckoo,' and 'After dinner, I worked bread, then came and mended stockings beside William; he fell asleep,' the glory of a great poet's development gives to these simple touches a value that later students thankfully recognize. One whose experiences of life have been gained on a much lower level can only hope at best for the patience of an idle reader in a leisure hour. Of Cambridge in particular it is not easy to write with freedom and at the same time to avoid fulsome praise or partisan malignity. To be 'spicy' is not difficult; but, the more a man cherishes opinions of his own, the more likely he is to escape vain regret by expressing them with reserve. For the same reason I have avoided reference to a personal wrong, admitting no excuse, received many years ago. Reference would only serve to relieve my own feelings, and would now be as unwise as Gunning's lengthy narrative of his affair with Dr Browne. But reticence and indifference are not the same thing.

My reminiscences of Cambridge begin just about the time when Leslie Stephen's *Sketches* leave off. It was that eminent man's fortune to illustrate the state of things while the residents were awaiting with mixed feelings the approach of Academic Reform. Much of what he says was more or less literally true of Cambridge life in my earlier years. Some of his remarks, e g those on Heads and Professors, are still deserving of careful consideration, in spite of all the changes that time has brought. I am not presuming to class myself with him. But I wish to record my sympathy with most of the criticisms implied in his pictures, and to profess my belief that I have been an observer of a very different scene from much the same point of view. With the opinions expressed in his *Early Impressions* I agree in almost every detail. I only wish I had had the good fortune to know him.

There is one subject, very interesting to me, to which I have made no reference in the following pages. The changes in the position of women during the last seventy years are so far-reaching that they must receive marked attention from future historians of England. When we reflect that they include the Married Women's Property Act of 1882, and the steps by which women have found their way into the House of Commons and Municipal Corporations, the Profession of Medicine and the Magistracy, not to mention their steady advance in other callings, we old people have food for thought. The helpless woman of the mid-nineteenth century has passed away. Men who can look back threescore years and ten have good reason to be thankful for a change of type that has made even the Anti-suffragist sister more of a human being. Nor need they fear that mercy and self-sacrifice are extinguished in the present generation through the coming of the New Woman. Those who remember the deeds of Florence

PREFACE

Nightingale have lived to be contemporary with
Edith Cavell and Lilian Starr. Woman has not
said her last word, or done her last deed of heroism.
At Cambridge it would be natural to dwell on her
patient and fruitful achievements in the field of
study, and on the spectacle of wise mothers
bringing up their children to walk worthily. But
Cambridge is perhaps the one place in the civilized
world where the topic of the Student Woman is
for the present best avoided.

WEH

February 1925

CONTENTS

NORFOLK—COLKIRK

I AM told that I was born on 21 Dec 1847 at Colkirk in Norfolk, a village 2½ miles south of Fakenham. My mother's family, the Brownes of Fulmodeston, were long established in the county; so far as I know, average specimens of the smaller landed gentry. They followed the usual course of their kind. Generations put together a nice little estate by means of judgment and thrift. Then the temptations of ease started them on the downward road, and the forties of last century saw a spend-thrift heir wreck their fortunes. Deaths left my mother heiress of what small remnant was saved. My father was the youngest of the five children of Major W P Heitland of the Madras Pioneers, who had served with distinction in the Mysore and Mahratta wars, and was one of the 'fiery few' in the battle of Assaye. Among the many godsons of the Duke of Wellington was my father, named Arthur after his father's old commander. Weakly and very thin, he was not trained for a profession, but put to 'learn farming' in Wiltshire. In the middle of the nineteenth century it was a common delusion that a gentleman-farmer could make a safe living, without facing the hardships of rustic life. In Norfolk, when living with a sister at Colkirk, he met Mary Browne, and they were married in 1846. Of this marriage three sons and four daughters were born, and two sons and three daughters reached full age. I was the first born, and have two sisters now (Jan 1924) living. We have branches in America and Australia.

The first thing I remember is the death of the Duke of Wellington, my childish attention being called to some pictures of the funeral procession. This was in the autumn of 1852. After this come a mixed series of recollections of happy childhood in our house and grounds at Colkirk, gradually extending to the village and to the market town of Fakenham. The Crimean War was felt even in our rural neighbourhood. The recruiting sergeant took away men. The inefficient Government wasted them. Well do I remember the dreadful accounts of the camps and hospitals at the seat of war, as my father read out the reports of the war-correspondents. Indignation was general. Ladies did all they could in the way of knitting scarves mittens and other things to comfort the brave fellows suffering in a Russian winter. I learnt to knit and played my little part. But I fear our products reached the men too late or not at all. Soon there followed the Indian Mutiny, with its own peculiar horrors. On a child just becoming conscious of the world such events made a deep impression, and the home-coming of a Grenadier Guardsman with an ugly wound was not forgotten.

The village of Colkirk is on high ground. The Church tower commands a wide view and has been useful to the Ordnance surveyors. The parish includes both light and heavy land. It is a healthy place, only troubled in dry summers by a passing shortage of water. In a Norfolk gazetteer of 1854 the population is given as 464 souls. The Census returns give 438 in 1891, 420 in 1901, 409 in 1911, 401 in 1921. These figures tell in brief the tale of village history. The 1300 odd acres in the parish were nearly all owned by large landlords, who lived elsewhere. There were some four or five substantial farmers, and I think two remaining small yeomen, the last of whom only succumbed finally after 1861. Others who had belonged to the same class were labourers for wages or had drifted away to serve elsewhere. Farm work was of course the main occupation of the men and of many of the women. The ordinary wage of a farm hand was 9/- a week, with long working hours. These people reared families, often large ones. That they managed to do so is to be explained partly by the early age at which children were put to work and so to increase the family earnings. But I am sure that this resource was not enough. Patient and honest as they generally were, it was true of them that hunger knows no law. As a youngster I was on friendly terms with many, young and old; and I remember being taught mysteries in the setting of snares and traps, which were ABC to my instructors and a delight to me. I recall too that when I undertook the collection of eggs at the farm it was strange how the hens

3

appeared to have left much of their duty undone. And there were always in the village a few idle or half-employed fellows whose means of living were not manifest, but who were certainly fed somehow. Looking back, I am not inclined to judge them severely: I have stolen food myself in my boyhood, with less excuse. There was more potential labour about than was needed, and the modern migratory habit was a thing of the future. I have heard a farmer remark 'We want a sergeant round here recruiting.' That was the most obvious remedy he could think of.

But the people were not all farm labourers of a merely general kind. On the farms there were marked distinctions of function and skill. Not to mention ploughing, mowing, threshing, sowing, etc, in which the use of machinery was only beginning on a very small scale, the old shepherds were notable characters. They were representatives of knowledge and experience handed down from generation to generation, and well aware of their own value. A visit to the folds at the season of lambing, and a talk with the shepherd, was a real treat. He lived for the time in a little hut on wheels, which could be moved each year to the place chosen. Lonely but ever busy, he bore his responsibilities calmly, an impressive rustic sage. Another specialist of note was the ratcatcher with his ferrets and dogs of wondrous intelligence. And the blacksmith and the carpenter were experts in the handling of bees. Nor

4

were these alone in possessing a knowledge of animals. The carter often had a peculiar understanding of horses; and I remember an old groom of singular veterinary skill. The owner of a brilliant Irish mare had found no professional Vet able to cure her lameness. He offered her as a gift to my father if he could only get her cured. She was sent to Colkirk, and the services of old Harry Dunn were enlisted. The old man produced his old books of records and prescriptions, written down by him long ago when he had been groom to an owner of many horses. From these he chose a treatment, and cured the mare so thoroughly that she was for years known as the best goer in the neighbourhood. At our sale in 1861 Strangleman the local dealer bought her for £60 and sold her again to Sir Willoughby Jones for considerably more. I could add further illustrations of the fact that rustic lore was going strong in those days, but this is enough.

Signs of change there were. The threshing machine worked by horse power was in evidence, but in course of being superseded by the steam engine. Yet I have seen men threshing with flails. T Chambers of the Hall farm was inventor of a sowing drill that served each seed with a drop of water. Yet I have seen two old-fashioned processes, broadcasting and dibbling. In the latter case, an elderly man walked between the ridges with a dibble in each hand, which he used to make

5

holes in the ridges. Two women followed him as he moved on, dropping seed into the holes. Steam ploughing was in the future, but the use of horses had almost driven out the slower oxen. I more than once saw ox-teams competing in ploughing matches, of course with a time-allowance. I never saw them again till I came across two or three on Wiltshire land in 1895.

But the difference between past and present comes home to me most clearly in the matter of village trades. The blacksmith and the carpenter are still there, but with a difference. They are more dependent on the large-scale industries elsewhere. Half-manufactured materials are carted up from the railway station or market town more than they used to be. Ready-made horse-shoes come from town forges, and the process of making them on the spot (which I have often watched) is probably extinct. The village blacksmith has now to be more of a mechanician and to be familiar with standard parts. The carpenter gets boards ready moulded from the sawmill, and so on. But when I was a child the bulk of the timber used was cut up in the old-style sawpit, worked by two men, top-sawyer and bottom-sawyer. There were at least two such pits at Colkirk, and the wood was mostly local trees. Of other trades we had a basket-maker, a tailor, a shoemaker, and a cooper. The last of these made the buckets and tubs not yet superseded by galvanized iron, and his chimney, lined with hooks

and bars, did a little business in smoking bacon
and hams. These village tradesmen were as a rule
thoughtful men of high character, a sort of
mental and moral aristocracy in the rustic society.
Modern machinery and concentration of industries
in towns have taken this valuable element out
of country villages: only the few indispensable
tradesmen are left. Gravestones in the churchyard record the names of the old generation
whom I saw in the last stage of the struggle for
existence.

The parish bore no traces of former open fields
and holdings in isolated strips. I suppose the agricultural reforms carried out by Coke of Norfolk and
others had made an end of such things. But there
was still a large waste heath or Common on which
the villagers could keep a donkey or a few geese.
Furze grew there, and this when cut and dried was
used for kindling. But this heath lay at the very
end of the parish, and only the cottagers living at
what was called the Common End could get much
use of it. No doubt bits of it had been stolen in the
past. At one corner of it there was in my time a
small hovel standing in an enclosed patch of garden.
Old people remembered that the occupant had
arrived many years before, camped on this neglected spot, and eventually become a 40/- free-
holder by undisturbed occupancy. I have heard
how he turned his political rights to account in the
days of bribery and beer, when the county polling

7

was kept open for many days on end and votes were votes. The Common has since been enclosed and divided in the usual way among the land-owners, a plan which I leave the Economists to discuss.

The houses of the village were nearly all cottages of various quality. The better ones, built of brick and tiled with the heavy curved tile of East Anglia, were decent dwellings well suited to their purpose. Some of a more ancient type were smaller and rougher, the walls low and thick, built of flints bedded in mortar. The worst sort were those whose frame was really rough timber and wattle-work daubed with clay: roof high pitched, and covered with thick thatch, in which was the bedroom lighted only by a very small window in the gable end. These hovels easily fell into decay and ruin, and are now gone, unlamented. No doubt the overcrowding and discomfort in the cottages was extreme, but the people spent most of their lives in the open air, and made shift with what was to hand. A real difficulty was fuel. Wood was never plentiful in an arable district, and the spare sticks got in the thinning of copses or trimming of hedges were of no great fire-making power. Coal, occasionally hawked round by small dealers, was very expen-sive and beyond the means of many. Hence parish allowances to the poor often took the form of coal. The old-fashioned brick ovens were heated with faggots. For baking still went on in the village: the

8

baker's cart from the market town had not yet
begun its rounds.

Many marks of olden time had already disappeared. The site of the former village pound was
known, but the pound was gone. There were no
stocks. Indeed the only set of stocks that I remember
in the district were those on the green at East
Rudham. My mother remembered the 'Poor's
cottages,' two wretched little hovels occupied by
paupers rent-free, but these too were gone in my
time. The old roads and lanes were as a rule bad,
but the present road to Fakenham was a recent
improvement, and was still called the New Road.
Footpaths through the fields were many, in particular that by Testerton to Ryburgh was and still
is a charming walk. The railway from Fakenham
to Norwich was new and the service not very
efficient. Market trains were made up chiefly of
open trucks, in which the people sat on their
baskets or stood according to the room available.
I have known a train delayed for two or three hours
on the line between stations while an engine was
fetched to take the place of one that had broken
down. In those days it was supposed that the first-
class passenger was the important person, from
whom the companies were to earn dividends. Third-
class carriages were marvels of discomfort and dirt.
Those who used them treated them as passengers
despised and barely tolerated were tempted to do.
This damaging and befouling went on all over the

kingdom for many more years. But I can now travel with more ease and comfort third class than I could first or second in my boyhood. Unhappily improved railway services do not increase the prosperity of villages. Modern conditions have reduced or destroyed another industry that I remember still in full swing. Colkirk it is true had neither windmill nor watermill, but there were many of both in the neighbourhood. The sails of the former were a feature of the landscape; the sound of water-wheels was a frequent accompaniment to the mild flow of the Wensum. Steam power has now stilled or silenced many of these slow old enterprises.

The most important event in the general round of village life was of course the harvest. The work was treated as a sort of contract job, and I seem to remember that it carried a special wage (£5, I think) for the whole process, ending with the stacking of the crop. Labour was a matter of great strength and skill. A team of mowers, ten or twelve men in the prime of life, cutting their way through a large field of wheat, was a fine sight. Each man had his own proper place in the order and kept a regular distance from the man before him. I never heard of a scythe-accident occurring, and the ten or twelve swathes lay across the field with wondrous regularity. As each man ended his swathe, he slowly marched back to the part not yet cut, and the course began again. If rain seemed threatening, the scythes would be laid by for a while, and the men would bind the cut corn in sheaves then and there. Anyone who has tried scythe-work may guess what a toilsome job all this first stage of the harvest was. Yet the men, poorly fed, never faltered. About noon they rested for an hour and ate their simple meal, brought by children or wives. The Master (a name not then disdained) would visit the field during the day. If a stranger came on the ground, he would be greeted with a cry of *Largess*, and had to find a subsidy for procuring beer.

The usual stages of piling sheaves in shocks, loading on carts, and conveying them to the spot chosen for stacking, then followed. Stack-building was skilled work, growing harder as the stack rose. Most striking was the scene at a point when the stack was already high and the load on a cart was already half delivered. The man on the cart picked up a sheaf on his fork and tossed it to the man on the stack, who caught it deftly on his fork and passed it to another, who put it in its right place on the stack. The speed with which this process was carried out was amazing, and I have known it kept up till eleven o'clock at night. Neither darkness nor the strain of such protracted labour seemed able to stop the men's exertions. They were working by the job, not by the hour. The stack, duly built to stand and await the turns of the market, was handed over to the thatcher, a very self-conscious specialist then still in existence. His work had to last until a perhaps distant day when the corn would be threshed. This event was to me a day of joy, for the lifting of the last layers of the stack drove out the inevitable rats, who had an evil time of it, boys and dogs being ready to receive them.

Two sequels must not be forgotten. The Harvest-Home supper was a living tradition. My Father, though losing money all the while, dealt liberally with the custom. All the men and their wives brought fine appetites and goodwill. I remember a specially provided barrel of strong ale on one occasion, and the recognized duty of drinking it out. This was ably fulfilled. But the wives got their husbands home somehow, and I think that, considering all things, the voice of censure was rightly dumb. Gleaning was a matter of interest to the women. There was some dim tradition of a general right of gleaning over all farms in the parish, probably a survival of a village community long ago. But my Father insisted on keeping the gleaning on his farm for the wives of his own men. It was indeed a pitiful little perquisite; just what the rakes had missed, and no more.

In no department of parish life is the change within my memory so great as that in matters of religion. Let me quote again from the local 1854 gazetteer. 'The Church......is a rectory..... valued in 1831 at £805. It has been enjoyed since

1816 by the Rev Ralph Tatham DD.' Whether this valuation included the living of Stibbard, is not stated; I fancy it did. The two rectories were in the gift of the Marquis Townshend and were then held together. Dr Tatham, Fellow and Tutor of St John's College Cambridge, had received this benefice from the goodwill of the patron, his former pupil. Such was the mode of patronage in those days, and of course the Rector was non-resident in two parishes. The payment of curates left a nice margin for the Rector, which he continued to 'enjoy' after his election to the Mastership of St John's in 1839, till his death in 1857. This was quite regular in those days, when the blessed eighteenth-century expression 'Preferment' was still the note of public life in Church and State, and the judicious use of patronage a leading factor in the predominance of the upper classes. At Colkirk there was a large Rectory house awaiting a resident Rector. At one time the Rev Thomas Tatham occupied it as his brother's curate: by all accounts an eccentric old gentleman, for whose requirements the Rector was thus able to provide. His death left the Rectory as it was in my time, shut up for nearly all the year, open for a few days at Easter, when Dr Tatham came to draw his tithes and take part in a service. After Morning Prayer he stepped out first to the Church door and shook hands with members of the congregation as they filed out. That is, until my father and mother came

13

by. For he kept hold of my mother's hand, shaking it all the while as he greeted the rest of those passing. This ceremony over, he pressed my parents to lunch at the Rectory, where his sister took the head of the table. I well remember being taken as a child to pay my respects to the old bachelor and maid, who sat in two separate rooms. But children are apt to find stale dignity uninspiring.

It was all very proper, and also profitable, a good specimen of an ecclesiastical system untouched by religious warmth, and aspiring only to decorous tenure of emoluments. When the old man died in 1857, news came that at Cambridge no Will had been found, and that search must be made at Colkirk Rectory. Search was soon narrowed down to a certain cupboard in which was a sliding panel at present stuck fast. This was forced open by due authority, disclosing nothing. So a considerable estate had to pass by the procedure used in cases of intestacy. Neither College nor parish got a share of the emoluments accumulated in the course of a long and decent incumbency. But I believe that the village school at Colkirk was started by Dr Tatham in his later years. The cure of souls was delegated to W A Chapman after the death of Thomas Tatham. At first he lodged two miles away at Hempton and visited Colkirk on foot. Then he had a lodging in the parish, and eventually a small house that belonged to the farm rented by my father, where he spent the rest of his life. He

14

was a man of genuine piety, devoted to duty according to the Evangelical models of the day, and beloved for the constant exercise of all the gracious and friendly offices that a resident parson is in a position to perform. Having some small means of his own, he could put up with a poor stipend. But as a mere curate he had no power, and he was almost stone-deaf. This infirmity was a grave drawback to his usefulness. Intimate friends could shout what they had to say into his ear, but to his humble parishioners the necessity of shouting was a difficulty in the way of seeking advice. Moreover deafness so extreme, cutting him off from catching the pronunciation of others, rendered his own utterance very abnormal. A dreary monotone, in which consonants lost their force, made his speech hard to understand, and in the pulpit it was no easy matter to follow him. In short, the goodness of the man was his one asset. But that was much.

The state of the Church told its own story. The nave was filled with old shabby pews in every stage of neglect, only set off by one more modern, made of deal and grained in paint. This was our pew. Facing it were the pulpit and reading desk, mean structures, economically painted long ago. Evidently the painter had run out of paint, and it had not been thought worth while to mix more. So a large bare patch was partly covered by a large-print copy of the Degrees of Matrimony. This attracted my childish notice. Sundays went by in the course of the ecclesiastical year: many details varied in the service, but no change modified or suspended the momentous rule forbidding me to marry my grand-mother. As I had no grandmothers living, the prohibition did not touch me, but I was left wondering how it presented itself to others not exempt from the suggested temptation. Below the reading desk stood the parish clerk with his right foot on the floor. His left knee rested on the step leading to the pulpit. A rude board held his service-book. On a corner of this his predecessor had been used to lay his quid of tobacco when he took it out to make responses. Beyond these erections was the Chancel, empty and cold, and indicating the parsimony of former Rectors by the meanness of its roof, which was covered with common slates, contrasting unhappily with the old lead roofing of the nave. Of course all the inside walls shewed nothing but mouldy whitewash. At the west end was a gallery probably dating from near 1700. On its front roughly cut was the inscription

Edward Nelson built neither a church nor a steeple but a singing place for the people.

In this gallery several men used to assemble, bringing various instruments and leading vocal action with a skill more or less precarious. The clerk left his desk and joined them, giving out the psalm in due form, reading two lines at a time. But some-times a false start would be made, pitch-pipe not-withstanding. I have known the psalm to be changed in consequence. And my father recalled one occasion on which the clerk varied the formal announcement thus 'Let us *endavour* to praise God by singing ......' As there was no choir and no training, the wonder is that the singing ever got through without mishap.

Church affairs and practices being what they were, it was only natural that the pick of the parish should be Dissenters. All the more, as East Anglia was a special home of Puritan tradition, and had in its day been well represented at Naseby and Marston Moor. True, things had changed since then. The trail of the eighteenth century was marked in the conditions of religious life. Earnest piety, Puritan or Catholic, tending to ruffle the serenity of the classes in possession, was viewed askance by the Bishops on whom the choice of Kings and Ministers fell. 'Enthusiasm' was its name, despised yet dreaded. But official discouragement could not wholly quench it, as revival movements proved: and in Norfolk the Puritan survival was strong. A pathetic trust in individual interpretation of the English Bible was widespread among the village folk, those of them who could read. I remember having to visit Eastwick the blacksmith, a fine old man of noble character, one Sunday. He rose from his great Bible, heard my message, and sat down to his Bible again. Such men, generally free from bitterness, could not adhere to a lifeless Church, and made their own religious arrangements. The

more emotional sort of Dissenters, usually called
Ranters, held occasional noisy assemblies, known
as 'Camp Meetings,' on a piece of open ground east
of the churchyard. This 'Camping Ground' was
afterwards enclosed by Mr Sweet. On Hempton
Green larger gatherings of the same kind were held.
I have seen a great crowd there, listening to a
preacher speaking from a waggon. What the moral
temper of the villages would have been without
these survivals of Protestant fervour, I do not
venture to surmise. I know that my father, a Tory
and Churchman, was well aware of the Dissenters'
merits. In a world of poverty and ignorance, he
saw that they were for the time the salt of the earth,
grotesque though some of their doings might be.

I am tempted to digress for a moment, and to say
a few words on the religious position in Norfolk as
being the result of past history. Superficial my
remarks will be, but not I trust a partisan perver-
sion of the truth. Whether the total population of
the county was smaller or larger in (say) the
fourteenth century than it is now, is not from my
point of view a matter of importance. That its
distribution over the area was very different then
from what it is now, is evident enough. What with
continental trade in small vessels able to use the narrow creeks of the north coast as well as Yarmouth
and Lynn; with land owned and farmed by more
owners in smaller holdings; with industries carried

on in farm houses on a small scale by both sexes; the villages formerly had a chance. Hence there were more of them, and for the good of their souls the wealthy erected and endowed churches to serve the numerous parishes in an exceptionally populous county. Many were connected with the religious houses that abounded in Norfolk. In due time these houses were suppressed, for good or for evil. This meant, among other things, a stimulus to the formation of large landed estates, for the men of influence secured most of the spoil. And this tendency was momentous: it was not easy for the 'small man' to thrive by the side of greedy neighbours. Still there were the churches in the parishes. But those hitherto served from monasteries had lost their priests. I suspect that many of the ruined churches, of which there are a great number in Norfolk, fell out of use for lack of clergy in the time of Henry VIII, and were in some cases left vacant afterwards. Again, under the Reformed system, the pressure of priests on penitents being relaxed, there was less inducement for lay benefactors to come forward, and the lesser parishes would be unable to keep up their churches. But the wholesale wreckage, the evidence of which stares us in the face on the Ordnance map, is even so not sufficiently accounted for. It must surely stand in some direct connexion with the decay of villages.

Within a radius of four miles round Colkirk there are the sites of four churches in ruins—Testerton,

Pudding Norton, Pattesley, Godwick. One, or at most two, farms now represent, with their cottage belongings, whatever villages may once have existed there. The same state of things may be detected elsewhere, even on the map. Clearly there were once pious founders to build churches in these places, and inhabitants, however few, to use and maintain them. All that has long been changed. Now, whatever interruption may have been caused by the Reformation, why did not a revival of these religious centres take place, say after 1660? I take it that changes in the land-system, increasing the number of large estates, were in progress, and that the class of small landowners was decreasing. The resident squire, on whom depended most of what was done in a small village, became a rarer figure, and there was no one left with means to spare for maintaining the little church. But what finally took most of the life out of the Norfolk countryside was the transference of home-industries to other parts of England. The hand-work of the farm house went northwards to be performed by machinery driven at first by water power in hilly districts, later by steam. Thus the women lost an occupation; woollen goods, no longer home-made and even sold, had to be bought and paid for; while the productive activities of the farm became exclusively agricultural. The change in the economic position tended to strengthen the hold of the big landowners; incidentally it led to concentration of the country-

folk in fewer villages. The movement has left its
mark on Norfolk in the formation of great parks
and mansions in the eighteenth century. A common phenomenon is the awkward relation of
church and village. The church is often at the
extreme end of the parish, and sometimes enclosed
in a park, convenient only for the great house and
its belongings. The village has been pushed away,
cottage neighbours not being welcomed. Tradition
sometimes records the later stages of the process.
I fear ancestors of mine at Fulmodeston were not
wholly guiltless in this respect.

To this condition of things the Established Church
of the Hanoverian period readily adapted itself.
To revive extinct cures was no part of its function.
On the contrary, the union of parishes, supplemented by plurality of tenures, was found a convenient policy, enabling patrons to provide their
nominees with 'benefices' on which it was possible
to live in comfort. This suited the great landlords,
whose patronage fell to their younger sons or relatives, or could be turned to account as a means of
political influence. The 'family living' became an
institution. It had its good points, but it meant that
promotion on the ground of devoted service in
poorly paid posts was in practice ignored. And this
suited all patrons: the Church was a kind of Civil
Service, an appanage of power, carried on according to the principles of the age. It became the
custom to make clergymen Justices of the Peace,

and there were still in my time several of these in
our neighbourhood. I remember our groom telling
me with bated breath of a man being severely
flogged by order of the Reverend M—. The story,
perhaps exaggerated, alarmed my youthful mind.
The clergy that I knew were not men likely to give
such orders. But this Magistrate was a 'man of
good family' of the sort referred to above. When my
father was made a J P, he was more than once
shocked at the harshness of his brother magistrates,
clergy among them, and I have heard him refer
to the subject with bitterness. Under conditions
such as these no wonder there was in country
villages much sullen discontent. Men were bewildered, and saw no way out of the situation. The
landlords were in power, and looked at everything
from their own point of view. The clergy, even the
best of them—and saints there were among them—
were so much concerned in defining the one sure
road to Heaven that they were of little present
comfort to the poor on earth.

In 1857 came the revolution at Colkirk, where
we had had neither resident squire nor resident
Rector. It came by change of patronage. Lord
Townshend had sold the advowson to Mr Henry
Hoare the banker, who was interested in Norfolk
and a leading High Church layman. Till his son
Walter, the famous Oxford oarsman of 1861-3, was
qualified for the charge, he put in as Rector a

man of the then new school. The Rev J B Sweet, a Devonshire man from Blundell's and Balliol, set to work at once. In the first week he had rough seats fitted up in the chancel for a makeshift choir, and put in a harmonium. Meanwhile Mrs Sweet gave a hasty training to the girls at the school, and by the Sunday all was ready for a surprise. The new Rector was to read himself in, and an unusually large congregation assembled for the occasion. Such an event had not happened for more than forty years (1816–57). In particular, the musicians were in full force in the gallery, to shew what they could do. But, when the singing moment arrived, the Rector, ignoring the clerk and the band, himself gave out the psalm, the harmonium began to play, and the new choir to sing. Words cannot express the general astonishment. But the shock to old custom was final. Opposition died down slowly but surely as the merits of a live parson were appreciated. Into the details of further changes I need not enter, nor can I trust my memory. The vigour and human sympathies of Mr Sweet overcame the prejudices of my parents, whose connexions were Evangelical. I can recall my father's glee when on a certain evening he went to see the Rector and found him smoking a pipe. The practice had been deemed unclerical: but the sharing of a common weakness brought the parson into touch with publicans and sinners.

In no respect was the change more striking or

more beneficial than in the relation of the Rectory to temporal and quite secular affairs. The new man interested himself in all questions of present well-being, sanitation, Poor-law administration, housing, every-day morals, and the many matters in which the ignorance and apathy of parishioners called for information and advice. He withstood landlords who sought to close old footpaths. When a stack-yard fire broke out at the Hall farm, he was quickly on the spot, teaching helpers how to help and working harder than anyone at the water-cart. What little was effected in the way of salvage was mainly due to the man with the cure of souls. But he was before all things a Churchman of the new school, and as such apt to ignore the moral services of the Dissenters to the long neglected parish. The indifferent were lured to Church, and congregations grew. But to set his face against the sturdy Puritan element was a pity, for it estranged from him some of the best people in the village, at least for several years. Mr Chapman, the curate now superseded, lived on at Colkirk, honoured by the Rector and often invited to bear a part in the services of the Church. He was beloved by all the parish, and his presence and cooperation smoothed the path of the zealous reformer.

I must not forget the restoration of the Church, soon effected by the energy of Mr Sweet, backed up by Mr Hoare. Removal of whitewash disclosed remains of mural paintings, of which record copies

were made with more or less success. These were
very interesting to me: but I never liked, and do
not now like, the tearing down of mural tablets
that were doing no sort of harm. I think these
things have an historical value. The Timperley
family, to which they belonged, were long ago
extinct in the parish. To fix up these quaint old
monuments outside on the north wall had a new-
broom flavour. However, a later enlargement of
the building on that side led to their being refixed
in a better place, under the tower. Norfolk churches
contain a vast number of these memorials, and
surely the interest of the past does not end with the
Reformation of the sixteenth century. Perhaps it
was inevitable that the revival movement in its
earlier stages should wear something of a priggish
character. Its later tone has I think been less in-
tolerant. It had many a case of disgusting neglect
to deal with in the parish churches of our neighbourhood, and deserves praise on the whole. One
extreme case is so unsavoury that I dare not record
it in English. My informant was the architect employed in the restoration of the little church. The
living, consolidated with a larger parish about
$1\frac{1}{2}$ miles off, was served by the parson resident in
the latter, who could not afford either to pay a
curate or to keep a carriage. He walked over on
Sundays to perform afternoon service, and he was
an elderly man. Igitur, cum saepe accideret ut
venter ambulando laboraret, periculum erat ne

inter ministrandum foede conturbaretur. quod ne turpiter fieret, vir officii valde studiosus immissis fabris latrinam in ipsa ecclesia pone pulpitum faciendam curavit. hoc consilio effecit ut, si res posceret, brevi secessu recreatus rei divinae operam dare posset. The case was so far as I know unique, but I have heard of others not quite so extreme from other parts of England, and have seen some queer things.

I would not seem to imply that the old-school clergy were as a body shirking their duty and responsible for such a state of things as I have referred to above. There were men of holy sincerity and unobtrusive virtue in some parishes, who shrank from no toil or self-sacrifice, working on the old Evangelical lines. Good instances were the incumbents of two Rectories in the gift of Corpus Christi College Cambridge, at that time a noted centre of Low Church piety. These were Fulmodeston and Thurning. College patronage was not always a success, as certain other parishes knew. A marked feature of the period was the interest taken in the conversion of the heathen, including Jews. I recall the Missionary meetings to which I was taken, the atmosphere of which was of a kind that the present generation could not understand. The modern missionary, to whose merits many modern travellers bear generous witness, is of quite a different type. But I feel sure that the good people of those days had no foreboding of the coming

change. Nor were the landed interests less blind.
The first alarm at the repeal of the corn laws had
subsided, and the possible development of cheap
sea transport was as yet unguessed. The throwing
of small farms into large, the introduction of
machinery, and the industrializing of agriculture
on a capitalist footing, were in progress. This
policy, under the lead given by Lord Leicester in
his model farms, was for the time the last word
of wisdom. Rents were rising, and big tenant
farmers seemed securely prosperous. Some of them
lost their heads and lived in extravagant style.
I remember one who not only gave lavish entertainments but kept a fine orange-house for the
supply of his table. This was an extreme case, and
cool observers shrugged their shoulders. This gentleman's death revealed his bankruptcy, leaving his
family destitute. A handsome cheque to his widow
from the noble landlord was worthy of the liberality
of Holkham. But the whole affair gave rise to uneasy talk around the countryside. Another case I
remember was one rather of shortsighted levity and
miscalculation in general. I was present at the sale,
which dispersed luxurious furniture and other belongings amid the belated comments of the assembled company. Of course the big farmers mostly
kept 'hosses and dorgs,' and some hunted: in any
case these tastes were costly.

Our own downfall was less dramatic but not less
sure. By 1861 it had become clear that my father

could not carry on the farm any longer. In fact his little capital was gone, and with six children growing up in a country house beyond the remaining means a crisis had to be faced. For some years past minor sacrifices had been made in hope to turn the corner by reducing the scale of living, but in vain. So my parents bowed to their fate, sold off the farm-stock household goods etc, let Colkirk House to a tenant, and stepped out bravely into a life-struggle with poverty, in which the devoted toil and energy of my mother played a noble part. Of the migration to Pembrokeshire I will speak below. It must have been a supreme agony in those days of ill-developed railways. But I was then at school, and bore no part in the journey. Before I close these few reminiscences of Norfolk, it may be in place to add some notes on the life at home from which we passed into exile.

Colkirk House, built in the early forties of last century, was designed as a residence for my mother's brother John Browne, heir to a nice landed property in Fulmodeston and adjoining parishes. Accordingly it included whatever was at the time regarded as indispensable in the way of use and comfort on the living scale of an average country gentleman. The house itself had considerable merits. Its appurtenances were large. A fine block included first-rate stabling, lofts, coach house etc. From the ceiling of this last, above the carriages, hung the sleigh. Hard winters made the use of this delightful vehicle a convenience and a joy. Laundry, brewhouse, dairy, soft-water cistern, deep well, coalhole, wood-yard, and a far-reaching system of cesspools, served to complete the self-sufficiency of the establishment. If departments that had better have been widely separated were in fact brought close together, this was only the usual case with country houses. A little was already being said about '*animalculae*' in drinking water; but nobody paid much attention to such warnings, and the undetected *bacilli* had things all their own way. I well remember the masses of stinking filth that were brought up on an occasion when it was found necessary to 'fy out' the well. But I do not remember that it caused serious alarm. Two large kitchen gardens and a paddock or lawn provided food for man and beast. Several shrubberies, and a pleasant flower garden with greenhouses, added to the amenities of the place. Spent in such surroundings, no wonder that childhood was happy and life full of interest. As one grew up, expeditions and visits to neighbours took one further afield. In the summer one glorious day was spent in a family trip to the sea, generally to Holkham, with a bathe and a picnic among the sandhills. Best of all was in some years the migration for a month to Cromer, which was then a delightful resort, not yet reached by railways, frequented by quiet people from the country. In those days there were more local fisher-

29

men than there are now. Beside the crab boats there were larger craft that went after herring or mackerel. All worked from the open beach. The smaller boats were simply carried up or down as they still are: the bigger could only be moved at all on rollers by the joint efforts of a number of men putting their backs to it on each side, a sight worth seeing. An event of interest, occurring at irregular intervals, was the arrival of a coasting brig or schooner bringing coal from the North. She would run ashore at the top of the tide, and all the available carts of the neighbourhood hurried alongside. All the men worked furiously, and the coal was got out with speed; so far as possible, in the space of a single tide. Such was then the method of laying in fuel along the open coast line of Norfolk. The vessel when cleared put to sea again without delay. In the fifties of last century the old lighthouse was still standing deserted on the edge of the cliff. This, and recently also old Sidestrand church tower, have gone over. Such is the fate of the east coast.

EPITAPHS ILLUSTRATING CERTAIN PASSAGES
IN THE TEXT

I. A self-conscious family [Colkirk, 17th century]

Lo Time—Pearle—Ey, a Rebus, which to thee
Speakes what I whilom Was, a *Timperley*.
Wing'd Time is flowne, So is yᵉ World from me,
A glitt'ring Pearle, whose glosse is Vanitie.
But th' Ey of Hope is of a nobler flight,
To reach beyond thee (Death), enioye his sight
Who conquer'd thee. Hence spring my hopes yᵗ I
Shall rise yᵉ same, & more, a *Timperley*.

[Tablet to Nicholas Timperley, who died 1658]

II. An ecclesiastical figure of the 18th century [Exeter]

To the Memory of George Lavington LLD,
Who having early distinguished himself
By a conscientious and disinterested attachment
To the cause of Liberty and the Reformation,
Was successively advanced to dignities
In the Cathedrals of Worcester & St Pauls,
And lastly to the Episcopal Chair of this Church.

Endowed by Nature with superior Abilities,
Rich in a great variety of acquired Knowledge,
In the study of the holy Scriptures consummate,
He never ceased to improve his Talents,
Nor to employ them to the noblest Purposes;
An instructive, animated & convincing Preacher,

A determined Enemy to Idolatry & Persecution,
A successful Exposer of Pretence & Enthusiasm.
Happy in his services to the Church of Christ!
Happier, who could unite such extensive cares
With a strict attention to his immediate charge!
His absences from his Diocese were short & rare;
And his Presence was endeared to his Clergy
By an easy access & a gracefull Hospitality,
A winning conversation & condescending De-
  portment.

Unaffected Sanctity dignified his Instructions,
And indulgent Candor sweet'ned his Govern-
  ment.
At length, having eminently discharged the Duties
Of a Man, a Christian, & a Prelate,
Prepared by habitual Meditation
To resign Life without Regret,
To meet Death without Terror,
He expired, with the Praises of God upon his Lips
In his 79th year. Septr 13th 1762.

[A set of tablets the lettering of which is very fine]

DEDHAM

It must have been in the year 1858 that I was
sent to school at Dedham in Essex. The Grammar
School there was an old foundation, slightly endowed, which could be kept going fairly well under
conditions that were then rapidly passing away.
But the little town and its surroundings, famed
through the art of Constable, was peacefully stagnant
since the railway had left it aside. There was much
beauty in the neighbourhood, but the climate was
sometimes trying, for the low meadows were always

damp. Hot weather was apt to be relaxing: in winter the overflow of the Stour would lay a wide area under water, and a frost turned it into a vast stretch of ice. Somehow, with periods of sick-room, I got through three years of school life there, and escaped drowning in the river. If this was due to my being destined to another fate, the alternative is still in suspense. But looking back I marvel that in a place where the control of boys out of school hours was supremely difficult, and the temptations to boyish adventures ever present, no grave accidents occurred. Dedham was one of the places, not rare in the East country, in which there was an endowed Lectureship, a survival of old Puritan piety. I think it was worth more than the Vicarage. It had for some time been usual to appoint as Lecturer the retiring Headmaster of the School. In practice this meant a pension for a sound Protestant, the electing body being naturally of that colour. But the then Headmaster, the Rev G T Lermit, was a High Church man, and when he eventually resigned he was not made Lecturer.

Lermit had no easy task. The school could not pay its way on the support of local families. To attract and keep boarders from outside was the only chance of success, and attractions to other schools were steadily increasing. In later years he told me that he had saved no money out of his time at Dedham, and I cannot doubt it. What he gained was a home and the means of educating a

large family. Rigid economy had to be observed
in all household arrangements, and it certainly
was. Now boys do not as a rule mind roughing it
a bit, nor was there much to grumble about, save
in the way of feeding. Truth compels me to say that
the meals were not good. We got what the servants
thought good enough for us, prepared in a slovenly
and unappetising manner. Even our boyish hunger
sometimes revolted at the food, however good the
quality of the materials may have been. Hence
great importance attached to pocket-money that
quickly wasted in the grub-shop, and the eager
expectation of hampers from home with solid
dainties to be shared with friends. A cold plum
pudding well boiled was a treasure. I have known
one smuggled up into a bedroom: you sat up in
bed, devoured a huge slice of it, licked your fingers,
and turned to dreamless slumber with all the con-
fidence of youth. How to invest the last penny of
pocket-money to the best advantage was a problem
of agonizing interest. I remember that a penny-
worth of coarse brown sugar offered a plausible
solution: you couldn't eat it all at one go. Nor dare
I dissemble the fact that it was unsafe to leave edible
matters within our reach. I confess that in my time
I stole eatables, even potatoes, destined to be fried
for supper in a frying-pan owned by an unregistered
company.

We boys were a very mixed lot. Private connexions had enabled Lermit to draw some pupils

from families of good standing, lads who would have been a credit to any school. I remember three French boys (Lermit himself was of French extraction), four bold Australian brothers, two athletic brothers from the banks of the Orwell, one or two of military families, a contingent from Norfolk, and a very active and varied party from London. But necessity led to the inclusion of a less eligible class, boys with something wrong in their record, who had for some reason not been sent to school, or had been withdrawn from a former school. The younger of these could not do much harm, but those who stayed on at Dedham or who came later in life than most boys, were an undesirable element. What bullying there was (not very much) came chiefly from this class. One case I well remember. A big fellow of sinister appearance, who had left a well-known public school rather suddenly, was added to our numbers. We instinctively disliked him, but he became an object of interest and some sympathy when it was whispered that he was plotting to run away. The strictest secrecy was observed, and those who had any article that might be of use in his adventure hastened to offer it to the hero of the moment. I contributed an old flask that I had not the means of filling. He set out in due course, was recaptured next day, and restored without delay to his disappointed relatives.

The school teaching was not of a very high order. No doubt the salaries were not such as to attract masters of the highest qualifications. But the mechanical methods of those days were largely to blame. The masters did their best, and of one, W F Rawdon of Wadham College Oxford, I keep affectionate remembrance. Lermit himself was a born teacher. When he stood chalk in hand before a blackboard, taking a class in elementary mathematics, he was at his best. I only wish I had had more of his teaching. But I got pushed up in school, the intellectual standard of the boys being low. In the latter part of my time I was one of four in the head form. Two of them were elderly boys of respectable dullness, one a clever dare-devil youngster, far too bright for his company. If I am rightly informed, none of the three came to much good. Meanwhile examinations had to be so manipulated as to keep up the credit of the two elders. Such are the difficulties in small local schools where competition is weak. Lermit was not blind to the coming claims of Natural Science. He set up a small chemical laboratory, and now and then fetched a lecturer from London to deliver an address on some elementary scientific subject. This was well; but he could not afford to keep a regular assistant to teach chemistry, and the laboratory was soon disused.

My experience of the discipline was thorough. I cannot say that it was a great success. It was severe but not corrective in most cases, including my own. The cane was ever in use as a weapon of punishment, and occasionally the birch. The latter was supposed to be more ignominious, but nobody cared about that. It was less painful than caning on the hand (I speak as an expert), and the operator as well as the patient was liable to suffer some loss of dignity in the scene. If moral effect was the end in view, it was a failure. Hand-caning was painful, and Lermit made you share the pain he felt in inflicting it. A severe 'six-on-each' left your paws tender for weeks after, scored with blood-marks. The worst point about the corporal punishment was that it was often not the reward of a particular offence, but cumulative. Each master had a punishment-book in which he entered all the little impositions laid on offenders in the course of the week. Each Monday he reported to the Head the offenders' names and the number of times each occurred in his book. If your name were down three times in the masters' books all taken together, you got a bonus in the form of a caning. Thus, if you were set to write fifty lines for giggling in class, the matter did not end there. You were one third of the way to a caning, and it was only too easy for a boy with a sense of things ridiculous to make up the other two thirds. The duller the safer, was how the system worked in practice. But there was one undesigned result. Hard hands suffered less than soft, and it was found that hardening could be attained on the fives court, which was popular. On me (I cannot speak for others) the use of the

37

cane had a downright bad effect. It made me pit my wits against my pastors and masters, who little suspected the wide difference between appearances and reality in the ways and doings of a deliberately secretive boy. For instance, I remember one evening some of us wanted to bring in some illicit beer for an illicit supper. Competition was more in evidence for consumption than for transport, so I volunteered for the service. I got over a gate, reached the Pub, carried off the beer in a huge stone bottle on my back, and prepared to pass the Headmaster's door, which it was long odds would be shut. Just as I came abreast of it, he appeared in the doorway, saying good evening to a visitor. Yet I slipped past unnoticed and delivered my cargo safely. So efficient was a slight disguise, aided by a successful imitation of rustic gait and bearing. I mention this not because what happened to me is of any interest, but to illustrate the effect of Dedham discipline on a rather delicate and timid boy.

A good institution, which might have been worked to more advantage, was drill. Under the worthy old sergeant Jones we were put through evolutions as a corps, and also exercised with dumb-bell practice. The training might have been popular enough, had it not also been in use as a form of punishment. Extra drill, chiefly imposed on those who had been late for morning prayers, was a hateful performance. To parade with rifles, real or sham, had a grown-up air, and those were the days

of a Volunteer movement. The recent Indian
Mutiny, and doubts as to the designs of the French
Emperor, caused some uneasiness in England, and
at Dedham as elsewhere stalwart patriots met for
their occasional training. Dancing lessons under a
visiting teacher were a failure. Very few of us could
swim, and bathing in a shallow part of the river
was not much to boast of. Boating was of course
forbidden, and boats were a rarity. This meant that
the lure of the illicit was irresistible, only checked
by our financial difficulties. I remember being one
day warned, just after getting afloat, that Lermit
was approaching in a trap along the main road.
We slipped into hiding under the old pile-bridge,
and let the Headmaster drive unaware over our
guilty heads. So we had our fun, and the cane had
a rest. On the whole, with games and expeditions
in the pleasant country round, we gave ourselves a
pretty good time. Local residents were kind to us
young sinners, and I retain generally pleasant
memories of Dedham. My last visit was in 1911,
and it was melancholy to find that the old school,
closed some years before, had not then been revived.

A DIGRESSION

Let me turn aside for a moment to jot down one
or two details connected with a matter that may
seem to bear no relation to the life of an English
schoolboy in the sixties of last century. I mean the

American Civil War of 1861–5. How nearly Great
Britain got into grave trouble with the United
States is perhaps hardly realized by many of the
present generation, though the affair of the *Alabama*
claims is duly recorded by historians. But at the
time even a schoolboy could not help receiving
every now and then impressions of the great struggle
going on beyond the Atlantic. Boys are naturally
interested in a fight of any sort. While I was at
Dedham the great prize fight of Sayers and Heenan
took place. Our excitement was intense. The first
copy of *Bell's Life* was eagerly seized. We all rushed
into the big schoolroom, settled down in orderly
silence, and a boy with a good voice read out the
report of the battle. Groans and cheers at critical
points led up to a final cheer for Sayers, and the
meeting broke up into pairs, who set to work
punching one another's heads, as an easy way of
letting off steam.

A great and bloody war far away was a very
different matter, but in the American case there
had been various influences operating to make the
conflict interesting even to a boy brought up in
Evangelical surroundings. I had been taught that
slavery was a wicked system, and had been encouraged to read *Uncle Tom's Cabin*. On the other
hand the propaganda conducted in this country
through 'Nigger songs' representing the slaves as
light-hearted and happy beings, on the whole well
off and contented with their lot under kindly

masters, had hardly ceased. Snatches of these songs haunt me yet. One day at Dedham a large negro appeared on the playground, and we boys inspected him curiously. He did not seem very happy. He pulled up the leg of his trousers and shewed us horrid scars about his ankles, explaining in broken English that these were marks of the fetters from which he had escaped. Genuine or not, his exhibition did not suit very well with the nigger songs, but was fully in keeping with Uncle Tom. Meanwhile one became gradually conscious that a number of respectable grown-up people sympathized with the South. One heard it said that the Southerners were gentlemen and knew how to behave themselves, while the Northerners did not. And we had not the knowledge to detect the misrepresentations of fact that underlay this persuasion. So our interest in the war could not rise above the mere pleasure of looking on at a fight and getting news of victories and defeats. For instance, I well remember seeing a master holding a newspaper and rushing up to him 'oh Mr Rawdon sir, please has the *Merrimac* licked the *Monitor*?' The first trials of ironclads in war were then a subject of eager interest to many.

The result of this fight [March 1862] had a sobering effect on British impulses. There had been much silly talk as to the power of the British navy to break the blockade, and thereby end the war whenever it should seem desirable in the interests

of this country. Now it appeared doubtful whether
our great wooden fleet could successfully face the
new armoured vessels and the new artillery that
were being rapidly created in the Northern yards.
I was able to note the change of feeling, for I had
witnessed the bumptious spirit that some people
had lately been trying to foster. In December 1861,
on my way from Dedham to Tenby, I spent a night
or two with friends in London. I heard the impressive bell tolling for the Prince Consort's death.
But the leading event of the time was the '*Trent*
outrage,' and it seemed not unlikely that we should
shortly be at war with the Federal government,
whose officer had violated the neutrality of a British
ship. To amuse me, I was taken to the Alhambra,
then a 'variety' music hall where people supped
at little tables while a series of entertainments went
on. Leotard's feats on the flying trapeze were a
part of the programme. Also topical songs. One
of these included the following verses dealing with
the matter then first in the public mind.

> They think the British Lion sleeps,
>   but they'll soon find their mistake;
> aroused from his long slumbers
>   he'll savagely awake.
> He'll not succumb till from their flag
>   the insult out he wipes:
> he'll teach them that the Union Jack
>   can lick the Stars and Stripes.

And the cockney throng paused for a moment in
consuming Welsh-rarebits and stout to greet this

sentiment with a cheer. Yet this was long before
the days when the term *Jingo* put on its bellicose
signification. Well, the wisdom of Abraham Lincoln
prevented the foolish irritability of both parties
from running a disastrous course. But I never forgot
the scene I had witnessed, and from that time to
this have felt an ever-growing interest in American
affairs.

I do not think I need apologize for recording
these old memories of things that struck me as a
boy, phenomena to which the lapse of time has only
added significance. For the American Civil War
stands out in history as an event of supreme moment, politically, economically, socially, morally.
Its bearing on the history of our own country,
directly and indirectly, was immense. It was not
confined to the issues raised between the two
Governments, or such experiences as the cotton
famine which sent bodies of operatives to roam
England singing 'All the way from Manchester and
got no work to do.' It led to a growth of hostile
feeling in the United States that has only been
mitigated in recent years and is not wholly extinct
yet. But time and patient research have done much
to set facts in a true light. We can admire the
heroism and noble lives of Lee and Jackson and
others, and respect the motives that led them to
sacrifice themselves in a cause that could never
have been successful even through victory in war.
We can turn with disgust from the abominations

43

DEDHAM

of the Reconstruction period and the vindictive venom of Thaddeus Stevens and his crew. Above all, I hope we have learnt our lesson—that among the perils besetting our own country one of the greatest, ever present, is the inflated self-esteem, based on ignorance and guided by snobbery, that now and then tends to bring us into unnecessary trouble.

EDUCATIONAL FAILURES

Before I pass to reminiscences of Tenby, I must speak of unhappy enterprises in the sphere of education. From a clerical friend of Mr Sweet staying at Colkirk Rectory my father heard of the splendid Foundation at Winchester, and it was suggested that I should try for a Scholarship in that ancient College. Success would greatly relieve my parents by providing for my education. So in the summer of 1861 I was taken from Dedham to be examined at Winchester. But I had to compete in a Classical examination with rivals specially prepared by teachers who thoroughly understood what was expected of candidates and had put their pupils up to the niceties that were in vogue. A boy from a miscellaneous country Grammar School made a poor figure beside such trained competitors. A question in the Grammar paper, which I have never forgotten, revealed to me my incapacity. We were required to distinguish

$$\mathring{\eta} \ \mathring{\eta} \ \mathring{\eta} \ \mathring{\eta} \ \mathring{\eta} \ \mathring{\eta}.$$

44

Now of Greek accents and breathings I was deeply ignorant: indeed my knowledge of Greek in general was Shakespearian. But I stuck to my task and did pretty well. Daily lists of those still wanted contained my name until the last day of examination. But the end came, and I was taken home defeated. I liked what I saw of Winchester.

After the holidays I went back to Dedham. My Classical class-work was supplemented by private lessons from Mr Rawdon. But that good man was not really qualified for the task. At Oxford he had gained a first class in Moderations by very hard work, and he had a stock of artificial-memory forms designed to furnish him with ready material for use in the Schools. Such helps were wasted on a boy who needed development. They explained nothing, and left me bewildered, unable to grasp the why and wherefore, and so to apply what I learnt by the exercise of my own faculties. But I was devoted to the man. In 1862 I was just too old for the Foundation at Winchester, but there was still a chance of an exhibition there as a Commoner. It was arranged that I should try for this: if I failed, I was to try for the College Foundation at Eton, not being as yet barred there by age. I failed in both of these competitions. At Eton the custom was to post up each day the names of those not further wanted, and I figured in the very first of these lists. The jeers of Eton boys as one withdrew in manifest dejection gave me a sort of relief

45

reconciling me in my poverty to exclusion from a society in which such unfeeling demonstrations were possible. I had reason to think that my deficiencies in Latin verse composition were a main cause of my speedy rejection. But that was all in the game as understood in those days.

A long and weary journey to Bristol, and thence by steamer to Tenby, followed these disheartening experiences. Yet even in the hours of sea-sickness I do not think I ever believed myself the lifelong inferior of my more fortunate rivals. Nor did later experience at Cambridge contradict whatever self-confidence I had remaining.

PEMBROKESHIRE—TENBY

Tenby is an old fortified post, one of the chain that Norman conquerors put round the restless land of Wales. A large part of the ancient walls is still standing, and in 1861 most of the houses were within their circuit. It has a Mayor and Corporation, and a history. It is a beautiful spot. Perched on the limestone rock, with slates to the north and old red sandstone to the south, it looks down on two beaches and out over Carmarthen bay to the land of Gower. In clear weather the coast of Devon is visible. As our home of exile it was almost ideal. My parents no doubt found it a trial to start afresh in a humbler life, but they faced facts bravely. My mother began a course of sublime devotion to her family's needs. How she worked, no words can fitly tell. Among her labours was the making of the clothes for four daughters, not to mention herself, and often for her younger son. My poor father had no means of earning a living, and his part was mainly a passive one. But his character and social gifts had won him a good position long before our eight years of Tenby were at an end. To us children the change was pleasant enough. We had the sea at our doors, and that alone was a joy. And now that we were nobodies we were allowed a larger freedom.

Tenby was not a 'sea-side resort' in the ordinary sense, with piers and bands and long rows of lodging-houses. The nearest railway station was more than ten miles away, and the most direct communication was with Bristol by steamer twice a week. Practically all goods and some passengers came that way, and the arrival of the packet was an event of interest. The two boats were of very different types. The *Juno* was small, but noted for speed. She ended as a blockade-runner in the American Civil War. The *Firefly* Was a larger vessel, built for service in all weathers, and Captain Thomas was a representative sea-dog of the old school. She called at Tenby on her way to Wexford, and on her return trip the squealing of pigs on her fore deck could be heard some time before she dropped anchor in the bay. It was sweeter to come by her than to leave by her for Bristol. The railway was reached by coach either to Narberth Road (now Clynderwen) or to Pembroke Dock. The former service was very bad: a 'well-appointed four-horse coach' generally meant an ill-found vehicle drawn by three lamentable screws, and a well-grounded fear of missing the train. The Pembroke coach was rather better, but you had to cross Milford Haven in an open steam ferry and were liable to be drenched by rain. Then you started from the terminus, with so many miles more to travel. It was hard to choose between the two routes. The old broad-gauge South Wales railway was not prosperous, and the rolling stock was in bad order. A long journey on the line was a test of patience under discomforts of more than one kind.

These drawbacks had their good side from our point of view. First, the comparative seclusion of Tenby made living cheap. Rents were not high, prices of food in most items decidedly low. For instance, we got butter in the market at eightpence a pound, and soles were sometimes as low as fourpence. And so with many other things. As to houses, lodgings there were of course, but not in any great plenty: but there were a good many houses to be had at rent unfurnished. Such opportunities attracted families of limited means. Among them were some in much the same position as ourselves, unable to go on living in their country homes; others were Service men on fixed pensions, and a few residing in Tenby for reasons of health. Out of various sorts was formed a most pleasant society, cultivated and economical, not easily to be matched in any town of twice the size. The children found good company outside their own households, and enjoyed life thoroughly. Boys home from school in the long Christmas holidays of those days played football or hockey on the Burrows or the beach. But in the place itself education seemed to be forgotten. My father did his best to give his daughters some teaching, but his own lack of proper training was a difficulty. Missing his horse (for he was a good rider, and hunted in his youth), and having now no occupation, I fear Tenby life was a sore trial to him, at least until some of the residents set up an unpretentious little club. Of this he was a popular member, eventually secretary.

The little harbour, dry at low ebb, was then a scene of much activity on a small scale. A considerable fishery was carried on by trawlers, mostly from Brixham, who found their market at Swansea and elsewhere. On Saturday they came back to port, and the harbour was crowded with them, set up by their legs and bright with bunting. The crews generally took a rest ashore, and went to sea again on the Monday. Every space at the sides of the harbour was used to provide berths for local boats, from the then familiar Tenby luggers down to the smallest rowing punts and dinghies. Boatmen hung about, ready to take parties out for a sail, and one could always get a punt to paddle about in by oneself. All this is now changed, as I found

on revisiting Tenby in 1905 and 1919. The trawling
fleet is gone, apparently working nowadays from
Old Milford. Sailing boats are now much fewer,
rowing boats for hire fewer also. A minor fishery,
dredging in the bay for the large Tenby oysters, in
which some of the luggers used to be employed in
winter time, is now long extinct. I missed the old
race of boatmen who used to lean against the pier-
road wall waiting for engagement. They were
never in a hurry, and sought variety chiefly by
spitting alternately into the harbour and the road.
There were also a few seine boats. A rumour of
mackerel in the bay at once mobilized these,
manned by motley crews mostly of men whose
work was on shore but who were handy watermen.
I have seen immense catches made on the south
beach, and have hauled at the seine ropes. Mackerel
would then be plentiful beyond the local means
of disposal. I have known them at ten a penny,
and a quantity used as manure. On rare occasions
some strange fish would turn up in the bay, and
cause a little excitement. Such were an 'angel-
fish,' of which I have a sketch made by my father;
a shark of about 12 feet length, pulled ashore in a
dying condition on the south beach; and a huge
sun-fish, at the capture of which in the harbour
I was 'assisting,' as the newspapers say. The worst
of these prizes was that they were regularly turned
into temporary shows, and the liquidation of the
admission-fees demoralized the captors.

Carmarthen bay is a dangerous place for sailing craft with a gale from S or SW. All the inner or eastern part of the bay is shallow, owing to silt deposited by the rivers. No vessel of any size dare risk being driven by foul weather on that shore. The roads under the lee of Caldy island used often to be full of sailing vessels, mostly the coasting brigs and schooners of those days. One day the roadstead would be full; next morning empty. This place of shelter made wrecks a rarity. But if disabled a vessel had little chance of escape. And here I unwillingly must refer to a scandalous business transacted in Tenby harbour itself. A French barque of Nantes, on her homeward voyage from the west coast of Africa with 500 tons of nuts, lost both her captain and mate by sickness. Ignorant of navigation, the crew got out of their reckoning, and found themselves in the strange waters of Carmarthen bay. When nearing Tenby, some local seamen went out to them, offering to pilot their ship into the harbour, and somehow managed to gain their consent. Now the vessel was a light-built craft, designed only for deep water, quite unfitted to take the ground. An old seaman remarked to me that, once she came in, she would never get out. Being used to see colliers beached at Cromer, discharge their cargoes, and get away safely to the Tyne, I followed the proceedings with anxious interest. Brought in she was, to await orders from the owners in reply to a communication sent to

Nantes. But at the first ebb she was high and dry, and her seams at once began to open with the strain. In short she was a wreck, going more and more to pieces with every tide. Efforts had to be confined to salving the cargo. The local carters now took up the enterprise, exacting pay for removing masses of oil-nuts and storing them. At a place like Tenby such goods must have been almost valueless. In about three weeks the unhappy vessel was completely broken up and her materials sold to local adventurers for what little they might fetch. It is easy to guess what the owners' agent said on arrival in reference to the port hospitalities of Tenby. I heard that some of the stalwart Breton sailors drew knife on their tormentors. The town was honestly ashamed of the affair, but it was impossible to interfere in time, and so the whole disreputable exploit ran its course. Curiously enough, there were in the neighbourhood two ruined houses, of which tradition was current that in evil old days the families had been wreckers for profit, hanging out false lights: their sins had brought them to a bad end.

Just south of Tenby, between the high ground of the town and the Giltar cliffs, was a swamp. The water coming from inland could not easily drain away, and in the early sixties there was a sheet of water, shallow but permanent. On the sea front are sandhills, behind them on the way to Penally was a wild open tract called the Burrows, dear to naturalists by reason of certain rare flora and fauna; now much engrossed by golfers. At the northern end of the sandhills, next the town, it was and is impossible to prevent the drifting sand from blocking the natural outlet of the water. In our time a solid drain was laid, over which the sand could spread harmlessly, and the marsh land is much improved by the change. The main fact is that an old estuary has been choked. Traditions of boats passing up country that way must refer to long ago. Again, the shore between Tenby and Giltar point has undergone a marked change within my memory. Sand has gathered in vast quantity, and there is shoal water much further out than there used to be. Also the range of limestone cliffs from Giltar to Lydstep has suffered a good deal from the Atlantic waves that roll in on it with a south-west wind. It was a glorious walk along there on a blustering day, when the rollers boomed in the caves, and the spray swept inland, and here and there columns of water burst up suddenly through a blow-hole. But these little exercises of the sea have left their mark on the yielding rock: caves are beginning to give way at the inner end, and depressions walled round for safety betray the effect of stress below. The Giltar ramble, with the view over the sound to St Margaret's and Caldy, is one not easy to forget.

Passing to the North, there was no cliff walk, and the roads and paths led inland to the charming

53

little port of Saundersfoot in the NW corner of the bay, hidden from Tenby by Monkstone point. Nowadays there are more houses there, and visitors come in the summer. In the sixties the harbour was fairly busy with a small export trade of anthracite coal. Tramways of the old style, the rails in short lengths with fish-tail joints, brought down the loads and tipped them into the coaster schooners lying alongside the quay. There were several pits at work inland and the downhill run to the harbour was easy. In 1919 I found the quay-side deserted and only one tramway in use. Only one pit was working. An up-country walk revealed further signs of economic change. The small iron works by Kilgetty were no more, and an old tramway leading from a colliery further inland was in an advanced stage of ruin. The fact is that the coal belt running East to West through Pembrokeshire, formerly worked at many points, had ceased to be workable at a profit, and the coming of the railway had put an end to most of these local enterprises. And the progressive shoaling of the water near Saundersfoot made the shipping of cargoes there more and more inconvenient. I must not forget to mention the general use of culm as the local fuel, an important item of domestic economy. It was the 'small' and dust of the anthracite coal. Every cottage and farm-house had its heap of fuel ready for the winter. The culm was mixed with clay, and the mass trodden till the blend was complete, when it was stacked in a convenient spot. Fires did not blaze; but, when once lighted, never went out. Each night a thick coat of the clayey compound was laid like a plaster on the fire. By morning this layer was hard and hot, and served as an effective cooking-surface. This over, the fire was stoked down, and the top covered with balls of the mixture, formed by hand. These were dry and hot by the time the fire was again wanted. They lasted all day, and would bear the weight of a saucepan or kettle. In the Tenby kitchens of those days these cheap fires were common, and helped to keep down the cost of living; but I fear they are much less used now, owing to 'improvements' of modern date.

Of buildings that record the movements of the past there was no lack in South Pembrokeshire. The castles of Manorbeer, Carew, above all Pembroke, not to mention lesser strongholds, are a notable group. But I am not writing a guide book, and need not dwell on this topic. A special interest attaches to the so-called 'French Mills' at Pembroke and Carew (and I think elsewhere), as specimens of an attempt to turn local conditions to industrial account. In the middle of the county a number of 'pills' or creeks run down to combine in Milford Haven. Across the upper waters of some of these Pills a dam was driven and a mill built on the dam. The water-wheel, turned by the tide, furnished an intermittent but certain source of power. In the days before steam power these mills were no doubt

55

a remunerative and steady undertaking, but I fear they are now fallen on evil times. Their construction is traditionally attributed to a Flemish colony, known to have been planted in these parts. We have recently heard of proposals for returning to the use of tidewater for power by harnessing the Severn estuary. But meanwhile these old small-scale enterprises suffer from the change of conditions. The railway, at first thought likely to develope the fine harbour of Milford Haven, has ended by diverting most of its business to Fishguard at the cost of many millions. The activities of the Haven rise and fall with the fluctuations of Government policy in regard to Pembroke dockyard. Numerous forts of obsolete types look down on a generally silent waterway, records of Victorian days when the protection of this harbour was deemed necessary, to provide a safe base for the British Fleet. In the sixteenth century, when ships were of light draught, Haverfordwest at the head of one of the chief Pills was a port and a centre of administration for the maritime affairs of the district. But it is now a quiet market town with remains of a former castle. Old Milford, lower down near the mouth, was in 1875 an open sea-front on the Haven, with a small creek, Haking Pill, under it. There was then lying, beached in the Pill, the ill-fated *Great Eastern*. The hopes of fitting her again for sea came to nothing. After a few years at anchor in the Haven she was broken up. A large dock was afterwards formed by enclosing the Pill, but I hear that it does little business beyond serving the fishing fleet. Inside the Haven an oyster and prawn fishery used to be carried on by the Langwm fisherwomen. These tough dames used to tramp more than ten miles to Tenby, carrying their creels, and earned their living about as hardly as any people in the world. When a regatta was held at Tenby, a race was got up between two crews of them; for they were famous for skill with the oar. Then came a prize in money which was shared out. It may have occurred to them that their husbands need not be exposed to undue temptation: at all events they liquidated the windfall before starting for the tramp home. I remember that my mother, out in quest of ferns, found one of them lying in a ditch. To the question 'Are you unwell?' came a drowsy answer 'Buy a few prawns.'

I had almost forgotten the churches and clergy, and indeed they filled a much less important place than we had been used to in Norfolk. In the Tenby neighbourhood there were only three churches that I need mention. In Tenby itself the church was a notable feature, and the Rector, Archdeacon Clark, a much respected parson of the Low Church school. Piety and propriety were the notes of his incumbency; so much so that publicans and sinners seldom profited by the ministrations of a genuinely good man. No emotional revivalism or aesthetic allurements had a part in the calm decency and

57

respectability of the services. To the decent and respectable residents these conventional methods were congenial, but the mass of humbler natives belonged to dissenting sects. Penally, about two miles away, had an Evangelical parson of a more decided type who was noted for plain speaking in the pulpit. Officers from the barracks hard by, if they dared to be irreverent in church, were known to have been roundly rebuked by Mr Hughes. Gumfreston, a little further inland, had like Penally a church of the ordinary South Pembrokeshire model, but smaller. It stands in a secluded spot among trees. At the lower end of the churchyard are some chalybeate springs. There are very few houses in the parish, and visitors from Tenby are or were often a main part of the congregation. In the sixties the living was held by Mr Smith, an eccentric old gentleman interested in botany, to whom the ferns and other plants (even brambles) that grew on the church walls were a subject of pride. All manner of stories were told of his quaint doings in church; but archaeologists attracted there by certain architectural details spoke kindly of an 'original.' There is a great sameness about the South Pembrokeshire churches. Occasionally you find varieties of type, and Carew is remarkable for its fine tower. A good local specimen is Castle-martin in the south-west corner of the county. They differ widely from those in the northern part and Wales generally.

Into the changes that followed the death of Archdeacon Clark at Tenby I do not propose to enter. But while I am on Church topics I must say a few words about two churches in South Carmarthenshire that presented interesting phenomena. In the summer of 1866 my mother resolved to turn an honest penny by letting our house to visitors and migrating to Pendine on the Carmarthenshire coast. There we encamped in a cottage and lived the simple life. The doors of the rooms, made of the drift-wood that comes ashore on the surf-beaten beach, were full of holes bored by the well-known shellfish. The primitive village stands at the point where a stretch of encroaching sandhills succeeds the rocky cliffs. The church is a little way inland. The service was in English. Hot weather caused the door to be kept open. Pews in the old style were the furniture, and the floors of them had generally rotted away. But there was a good congregation of country folk, attentive and serious. The men usually sat at the outer end of a pew and spat into the central gangway. The parson, an old man but vigorous, walked to his duty several miles from another parish where he lived. He had a beautiful voice and uttered every work with marvellous ease and fluency. Services were short, owing simply to his amazing speed with no suggestion of irreverence. My father was delighted with him, but said he would back him to read the Creed quicker than any other man: in truth the congregation were

59

always a clause or two behind. To get a word with Mr Thomas was not easy: service over, he at once started off on his return tramp to Landawke. The open door had also its drawbacks. A kitten would come in and upset by its gambols the gravity of us youngsters. One day a pig solemnly came into the doorway and for a while listened to the proceedings with a critical air. When it gave a decisive grunt and withdrew, the devotional atmosphere was impaired.

In the next summer we migrated on the same plan to Laugharne, a decayed little port town some miles further east. It stands on the miniature estuary of the Taf, a river which has a 'bore' on a small scale and is not without danger to careless ramblers. It is a place of much beauty, and has one of the ruined Norman castles. Two old warehouses were then standing idle: whatever trade Laugharne once enjoyed had been cut off by the railway passing some four or five miles inland. But it still had a little Corporation and a Port Reeve. Houses were to be had at very low rents; which, combined with the general cheapness, led a few necessitous families to make it their home. So far well. But it also offered a retreat to undesirable persons whom their relatives were driven to seclude. One melancholy figure haunted the street at the time of our sojourn, an Oxford graduate of ability and good standing, ruined by drink. He was past the stage of a money allowance, and some Laugharne people were paid to house and feed him. He stared blandly into your windows, and you could easily believe the stories that were told of him and of others lately departed. Well, Laugharne was dead-alive enough, and the church unattractive, so we found our way to Landawke in hopes to come upon Mr Thomas in his other cure. And we were not disappointed. The little church, a genuine relic of the far past, deliciously unrestored, stood in a hollow, with a farmhouse and a manse hard by. Centuries of interments had raised the churchyard level, and you stepped down into the church over a notable threshold. It was a gravestone of the Roman Christian period, and is duly recorded in E Hübner's volume *Inscriptiones Britanniae Christianae*. The tower was in a ruined state, and on the top of it a self-sown apple tree bore a few apples. I have a sketch of it made by my father. A sister accompanied me to the service, and we were the obviously un-expected congregation. Three others were present, the parson and his daughter and the old clerk. It was a strange scene in the venerable darkness of the ancient church. The service was performed with characteristic smoothness, down to the point at which the clerk seemed doubtful whether this was one of the 'places where they sing' or not. He glanced up at Mr Thomas, who answered by a nod, and at once obeyed by singing in his cracked old voice two or three verses of a psalm. A short and fluent sermon brought the proceedings to an end.

A more perfect specimen of the isolation of country clergy could hardly be found. The farmer (church-warden) was a Dissenter.

And here my reminiscences of old Tenby and the country round must be broken off. In 1869 our house was wanted for conversion into lodgings, and we had to migrate once more to a new home. Many later visits to Tenby convinced me that the coming of the railway has not been an unmixed boon. The town is enlarged in the customary style of seaside resorts, and owners of land have no doubt profited thereby. A pleasure pier and other 'im-provements' testify to the outlay of somebody's capital; whether remuneratively or not, I cannot say. For the accommodation of lodgers and enter-tainment of trippers the place is 'developed.' For real residents, quiet family people, it seems less attractive than of old. But nature has done so much for it that human errors can never deprive Tenby of all its charm. For what it has suffered, the Governments of the past are partly to blame. The beautiful mass of St Catharine's Rock is a silent witness. Its rough surface with the little hermit's chapel on the top was a favourite haunt. In the later sixties this spot was at great cost occupied by a stone fort, said to be for protection of Caldy roads. It never was, or could have been, of any practical use, for the limestone rock itself could not stand the concussion of firing heavy guns. Its failure was in due time confessed by desertion, and eventually by sale to a private purchaser. In 1919 I found the approach barred, and a notice-board proclaiming the exclusion of trespassers. So the net result is waste of money and the loss of what was undoubtedly a public right of access. Such are the fruits of free and intelligent self-government and departmental wisdom.

APPENDIX TO TENBY CHAPTER

A PEMBROKESHIRE SQUIRE
[LAWHADEN CHURCHYARD]
To the Memory of
John Herbert Foley Esqre
of Ridgway in this County, who,
with powers to command and virtues to adorn
the Eminences of Life,
walked tranquilly along the Vale;
and was faithful to the purposes of his being,
though not elevated to the observation of the world.
With a rich and cultivated understanding,
subdued and regulated passions,
a heart glowing with benevolence,
and manners polished by a wide and early inter-
course with mankind,
He was Happy, Beneficial, Admired & Beloved;
correcting the false inferences of Ambition
by showing that
it is not the Amplitude of the circle,
but the Utility which it includes,
that is of consequence in the estimate of man.
The Relief of the Poor, the Succour of the Op-
pressed,
The Instruction of the Ignorant, the Delight of the
Friend,

and the Enjoyment of the Family,
he has left a void in society
which will not easily be supplied,
or quickly be regarded without regret.
His moral course, which began on the 10th of
Novr 1753,
was terminated
amid the sighs of his country, and the cheerings of
his own conscience,
on the 29th of May 1809.
For others whom its interest affected
it was unhappily too contracted;
for Himself,
embracing all the great objects for which it was given,
its line was sufficiently prolonged,
as its circumference was complete.

[Copied in 1865 by my Father from tablets still complete. In 1895 I found the stone badly flaked, but most of the inscription still visible.]

SHROPSHIRE—SHREWSBURY

In September 1862 I passed as a schoolboy into surroundings very different from what I had hitherto known, to the old school in the old town of Shrewsbury. There was then no Central Wales railway, and the journey from Tenby was not a simple matter. Ten or eleven miles by coach at an early hour, then railway to Newport, brought us to a frantic scuffle on the narrow and crowded platform. Luggage had to be found and put on an omnibus plying to the other station. Being of course late, we found there the Hereford train kept waiting, all the staff in furious impatience, and no chance of labelling our trunks, which had to be tossed in anyhow. So we crawled along to Hereford, where we had to change again. Nowadays one can hardly believe how great were the discomforts of railway travelling in those days of small and jealous companies. But we got through to Shrewsbury at last, my father even more tired than I. I was taken to Rigg's Hall, the house of the Second Master, where I had been entered by Lermit's advice. My school experiences must be kept for a later page. I feel bound to speak first of the old town, in which I have been deeply interested for now more than sixty years.

Shrewsbury is one of the most important of the Norman strongholds fortified to defend England on the side of Wales, and also as a centre of traffic and trade. Its position between Chester and Chepstow made it a sort of capital of the Welsh March. The Severn, till recent times a line of barge-traffic, makes a wide bend round the town. The narrow isthmus of high ground left by this loop was held by a castle of which a good part still stands, looking down on the railway station, placed on the neck for engineering reasons. The old town, perched on high ground and rich in towers and spires, is a fine sight from many points of view. Inside it abounds in picturesque corners, and has several fine old streets with fine old names. Sixty years ago there were many more of the overhanging timber houses than there are now, but some very good specimens are still left, better to look at than to live in. And to the casual visitor Shrewsbury is above all things a relic of ancient dignity. But those who explore the byways find a strange mixture not always pleasing. The extreme narrowness of some alleys is a quaint survival of medieval conditions, when security was the first consideration and led to excessive crowding in the limited space within the town walls. Antiquarian interest cannot preserve such curiosities for ever. But far worse are the comparatively recent lanes of mean houses, ill-built and ugly, that seem to cry for demolition. Here and there in these slums may be seen a bit of older and better type, such as the ancient Mint house, or one that was formerly the town residence of a county family: but in general the sights and smells are alike evil. When you are told that in the 16th and 17th centuries the Plague was a danger ever felt, and that the School had a country establishment to which it could and did migrate in time of sickness, you can well believe it. How recklessly Shropshire people lived in those days may be gathered from that frank record, Gough's *History of Middle*. Of the suburbs, the Castle Foregate is a squalid growth on the low ground north of the castle. Frankwell is a traditionally Welsh group beyond the Welsh bridge, containing some good Georgian and Victorian houses, in one of which Charles Darwin was born. The Abbey

Foregate is a pleasant part beyond the English bridge, a development of what were once the precincts of Holy Cross. But there are later extensions also, by which the pressure on the inner area is now no doubt reduced.

In this famous old borough there were many survivals of old customs remaining in 1862 and for years after. The ancient gilds, once numerous, had practically ceased to exist, but an old procession and carnival, known as Shrewsbury Show, was still kept up. The procession, with characters on horseback, passed between the Castle and the School, and was greeted by boys with discharge of catapults and peashooters from Schoolgarden wall. With unofficial language in reply, it wound its way through the town to Kingsland, a piece of common land beyond the river, on which the gilds used to maintain their several 'arbours' for feast-days: one or two of these were still standing. On this space was held a fair, in reality a merrymaking which degenerated into a licentious orgy in the course of the night. By decent citizens it had long been recognized as a public scandal, kept going to serve liquor-interests. But this opinion was ineffective until the chaplain of the gaol, an active Irishman, took the matter up and procured signatures to a memorial for abolition so quietly that the Licensed Victuallers were caught napping. Of course I never witnessed the scenes on Kingsland, school discipline forbidding curiosity; but the lurid descriptions that were current were attested by sufficient evidence. A more harmless and useful relic of old times was the yearly bacon and cheese fair, held in the streets. All down Pride Hill the pavement on both sides was covered with sides of bacon and large cheeses. Traffic in mid street was congested, but nimble folk such as boys could pass along the sidewalks, stepping from cheese to bacon, competing with dogs busy in improving the occasion. What brought this quaint survival to an end was the erection of the great covered market. This stands on the site of an insulated block of old buildings which I well remember, a regular rabbit-warren, picturesque but unsavoury, the refuge of small businesses and trades. The building of the new market was the first of the many changes for the better that Shrewsbury has undergone within my memory.

Of the parish churches only St Mary's needs special mention, not merely for its beauty, but because the School boarders had the chancel seats. St Chad's, the premier church of the town, was ruined by the fall of its tower in the eighteenth century. Contemporary taste shrank from re-building the old fabric, and in its stead erected an 'elegant and commodious' circular edifice on the model then in vogue. The removal of the original 'three-decker' has taken away from new St Chad's much of its typical Georgian character. St Alkmond's and St Julian's had been victims of the panic caused by the wreck of old St Chad's.

The body of the church was in each case demolished (with difficulty, it is said,) and rebuilt on an improved and hideous plan. The towers were left standing in grotesque incongruity. The noble Abbey church bore marks of its treatment in the successive periods of fanaticism and 'commonsense.' In all, Low Church usages prevailed, but the Vicar of St Mary's was beginning the methods of the new Anglican school, and in time effected a change that spread to other parishes. Of Dissenting chapels there were plenty, one of them Welsh. The Romanists had a good grip on the town, and are said to have gained ground in recent years.

But all these provisions for spiritual welfare could not be said to have had much obvious effect on the morals of the ordinary population in the latter part of last century. The slum folk had not much chance of decent living, and a small colony of indigent Irish did not improve matters. It is no slander to say that there was a deal of drunkenness and its attendant evils. And the country folk who came in to market often neglected to go home sober. Later experience of Cambridge led me to conclude that this is unnecessary, and I believe that Shrewsbury has greatly changed for the better in this respect. In the time of which I speak there were hardly any 'amenities' or provision for harmless amusements; popular education was in its infancy. The state of mind in which the respectable classes deplored the conduct of the disreputable, and passed on with a shrug of the shoulders, was prevalent at Shrewsbury as elsewhere. The long campaign against drink carried on by Mrs Wightman was in effect an Evangelical protest against the fatalistic English attitude of acquiescence in evils. In Shrewsbury at least there was one who refused to believe that social maladies admitted no remedy.

Among the changes that strike an old Salopian as most beneficial are the improvements in the Quarry and along the riverside, and in the control of the river itself. The Quarry, a public park with fine avenues of trees, had for centuries been a favourite resort of residents, whose promenades there Macaulay has described. Plays were acted in the Dingle by the school boys of Elizabeth's time. But it was after all a deserted spot, turned to little account. The suppression of the old Shrewsbury Show, referred to above, may have suggested the institution of something better in its stead: at all events the Shropshire Horticultural Society seized the opportunity of holding their yearly Show in the Quarry. This enterprise was a success from the first, and it is now perhaps the best thing of the kind in Great Britain. The position of Shrewsbury as a great railway junction helped the scheme. Gradually it became clear that much could be done to improve the Quarry itself, and its approaches also. Profits made on the Show were used by the Society from time to time for this purpose. Further space along the river bank has been acquired and laid out, and the town can today boast one of the finest pleasure grounds in England. Now improvement begets improvement, and in recent years the Severn has been taken in hand. In my time it was a singularly wayward and treacherous stream. In summer it ran very low. At certain points it was contracted into the 'fords' which many living can remember, so narrow that there was not room enough for the free use of oars on both sides of a boat. Weeds flourished rankly on the shoals and made steady rowing difficult. Little adventures gave variety, but regular practice in the noble art was liable to interruptions. In winter there were often floods, when Severn took charge of himself, and the arches of the Welsh bridge were none too high for their purpose. I remember one winter [1870 I think] when large parts of Frankwell and the Abbey Foregate were laid under water, and church properties in the Abbey church were rescued by boat. It was known that the floods were mainly due to the rise of the Vyrnwy, a tributary stream. When the Corporation of Liverpool dammed this river to supply their city with water, these sudden rushes were checked, and the Severn at Shrewsbury now represented more exclusively the drainage from Plinlimmon, that is the Hafren (*Sabrina*) whose name it bore. Engineers then took the business in hand, built a dam below the town, and turned the river for miles above into as fine a stretch of water as oarsmen need desire. Among rowing schools

71

Shrewsbury now holds a leading place, no longer hampered by the hindrances with which my contemporaries strove so long.

The above notes on the town are derived from three lines of connexion with it. I was a boy at the Schools from September 1862 to the summer of 1867. Our family moved to Shrewsbury in 1869, and my mother only left it in 1900. During those thirty years I was constantly staying there for many weeks at a time, gaining on foot or cycle a pretty wide acquaintance with Shropshire and its varied beauties, natural or artificial. Of the former no human folly can deprive it: as for the latter, let us be thankful for Ludlow and Wenlock and the peaceful border-stronghold of Clun. Since 1900 I have again visited many old haunts, and keep an affectionate memory of the historic towns and the hills of a lovely land.

THE SCHOOL

It is time to turn to the School—'Schools' is the proper title, of historic meaning,—as it was in my time. We boys took it as we found it: its past history was not then of much interest to us. We were not then aware that we were living among a host of survivals mostly dating from the time of Dr Butler, who had virtually refounded the old School, sunken in utter decay. When he left to become a Bishop in 1836, he bequeathed to his successor a famous

School and a long-established system. It was known that in his later years all had not been well with the inner life of the School. And I have been told on good authority that the powers of the great teacher had declined; he was in fact failing, and he did not long survive his translation to Lichfield. But of the merits of his system, elaborated in the early years of last century, few could entertain a doubt. Under the conditions of the period it had been fully justified by success. The school numbers are said to have been at one time above 400, and Butler made a comfortable fortune. He frankly warned Kennedy that the present prosperity was likely to be impaired by some changes of circumstances then in prospect. But Kennedy was not daunted. He became the new Head; and, being a pupil and great admirer of Butler, it was natural that he should follow his old master's methods. At the start this was no doubt well, but times were changing fast. To begin with, some undesirable boys had to be got rid of, and to keep up the total numbers was impossible. Railways were already making other schools more accessible, and the lines had not yet reached Shrewsbury. The accommodation for boarders had to be reduced, and the establishment maintained on a smaller scale. The financial depression was a hindrance to improvements, for the old endowment was too small and too much earmarked to bear charges of the kind. And Kennedy himself was soon lured by a friend into an investment that ended in disaster. Limited liability was not yet invented, and it is a fact that he had to bear a heavy burden year by year all the time of his headmastership. How great was the strain of this long struggle, was guessed by few. But it deeply affected his whole public life.

Nevertheless his triumphs as a teacher were beyond all question. That the Sixth Form took a fresh vigour in his hands was attested by the successes of his pupils during his earlier years, and loyally recorded by Munro in the first edition of his *Lucretius*, and by Bishop Fraser in his sermon at the opening of the new school in 1882. In this capacity he was unrivalled, but it was a 'one-man business.' In the middle of his career he was for a time disabled by serious illness, and the school declined. This I know on the best authority (Miss Marion Kennedy) and the 'Headroom Fasti,' a chronicle kept by the Praepostors, bears traces of the fall, as also do the lists of University Honours. In his later years there was a marked revival: he was no longer young, but his fire was still burning. The weak point of the whole organization lay in the comparative inefficiency of the rest of the staff. They were mostly good men enough, but not such as to initiate effective teaching by their own native genius for the work. And the traditional routine was sadly out of date. Reforms were beginning in the educational world, with livelier and more human methods of dealing with boyish minds. But

74

the mechanical and dreary grammatical drill made the Classics odious to the lower Forms. They were, as I can now see, Butler's methods without Butler, and in weaker hands they were inevitably sterilizing. Intimately connected therewith was a system of punishments unsurpassable in its folly. No allowance was made for boys' need of fresh air. The Butler tradition, hostile to games and sports, though dead, had left its mark behind, in spite of the rarity of floggings under Kennedy. The normal punishments formed a sort of tariff thus

(1) Penal Marks or 'Penals.' The unit was 50 lines from *Paradise Lost*. These had to be shewn up on Saturday, and each Monday the place for beginning was given out for the week, so that one could not write them on Sunday. The Punishments-master saw to this, and he sometimes accepted a number of Penals less than that due, on the ground of better handwriting.

(2) Two Penals = one 'Detention.' A Detention consisted in your being kept in half an hour after Second Lesson, from 12 to 12 30. You were supposed to spend the time learning by heart a fixed portion of the Latin Grammar, written in Latin as was then the fashion. On Tuesdays those 'detained' during the week were called up to repeat this to the Headmaster. Failure implied further punishment, but a tolerant management made this result rare.

(3) Two Detentions = one 'Idle List.' Idle List

consisted in your being kept in for an hour at least, compelled to bring work and do it then and there. But you had no further liability once the period was over.

The detentive forms of punishment were both evils, but the 'Detentions' had no redeeming merit whatever. An old penalty of solitary confinement in a sort of dark cage had ceased to be used in my time, but there were traditions of its use not many years before. The cage, Butlerian (or earlier?) still stood in the Fifth Form room. I do not remember gating as a Shrewsbury punishment. Flogging was done with a 'birch' of broom-twigs. A monitor was in attendance to lift the culprit's shirt. It was the right thing for him to place himself so that the more pungent ends of the birch caught his trousered leg and minimized the designed effect. The ceremony was of rare occurrence. As a sincere and final penalty it had its merits.

As I came to Shrewsbury when nearly 15, and had learnt something at Dedham, I was at once put into the Fifth Form and most punishments passed me by, the standard of ability there being low. Promotion to the Sixth in 1863 gave me a more than adequate experience of Penals, also of whole books of Milton to write out. No punishment of other kinds was used in the Sixth. It may seem strange that any punishment was needed there. But the tradition of effort and efficiency set going by Dr Butler had to be maintained. Examinations twice a year, with resulting changes of order, kept us up to the mark; slackness had to be punished; and the tone of the Sixth was on the whole excellent. Experience enabled you to catch this tone. An old hand knew how to deal with Kennedy in his various moods, and would never be punished, but a newcomer was apt to pay for his initiation. I have elsewhere in the *Eagle* (St John's College Magazine) for 1889, described the usual course of a principal lesson and its sometimes stormy phenomena, as the Doctor grew excited and his mighty voice resounded in the ample space of 'Top Schools.' What I must particularly note here is the speed and freshness of the lessons, largely due to the fact that there was very little reference to questions of formal grammar. There was a sort of assumption, quite unjustified, that a boy had all that at his fingers' ends by the time he reached the Sixth Form. When you understood how much was taken for granted, you learnt how to deal tactfully with passages out of which awkward questions might arise. A new hand would be less adroit. In earlier days to elude Kennedy's criticism was probably less easy, but in my time his keenness was often blunted by the wear and tear of long service.

In connexion with this matter of Sixth Form atmosphere I ought to point out that the record of Academic successes, which was rising again in his later years, owed no little of its brilliancy to those pupils who came from other schools to get the advantage of a year or two under the famous teacher. These had never passed through the tiresome mill of the lower forms: there were I think even one or two cases of a new boy being put straight into the Sixth. A number of notable names rise to the memory at once. Now it was not unnatural that such late-comers, some rather delicate, others unwilling to merge themselves for only a short time in the rough and custom-ridden life of Shrewsbury Boarders, should seek some special arrangement for suitable quarters. Some boarded with families in the town. But a peculiar plan was sanctioned at Shrewsbury, of allowing some of them to live in lodgings. For maturer students this plan did very well, and I know of no instance in which it was misapplied and abused until near the end of my time. In any fair estimate of Shrewsbury successes during the latter part of the Kennedy period, this important element of the Sixth Form must not be left out of account. It implies the powerful attraction of the Doctor's own personality, by the stimulus of which unselfish teachers in other schools desired their best pupils to profit. Incidentally it confirms my opinion that the work of the lower forms at Shrewsbury was by no means an ideal preparation for Sixth Form life.

The day-boy element (called Skytes) in the school was of very various sorts and values. None could be better than the best of them, sons of respected local families, or new residents of the same class. Here and there would be a boy of the right stuff, on the rise from poverty through high qualities. But it must be confessed that many were unsatisfactory, and tended to lower the character of the school. The old burgesses had enjoyed the right of sending their sons to the school free. It was held that the expression *libera schola* implied this privilege; and, though this interpretation was challenged by Kennedy and others, the privilege remained in use. But the sons of immigrants, not strictly burgesses on the old footing, were not easily to be distinguished from those of hereditary right. How the matter was finally settled I do not know. But I do know that a number of boys from the town were sent to school as a mere matter of course. Most of these had neither the ability nor the will to bear an active part in the competitive movement of the place as a centre of teaching. Some of them were kept on as schoolboys long after they had ceased to be able to profit by that condition. Of course this element was a serious drag on progress, a hindrance to a master's efforts: the Fifth Form in particular suffered from their presence. And to get rid of superannuated dunces, even in modern school-systems a problem, was exceptionally difficult when burgess-rights could be represented as being involved. I could illustrate this topic with true and significant anecdotes, but it is not necessary. And I must record my impression that in the removal of the Schools to Kingsland

79

the interests of the ancient borough were not sufficiently respected. As a non-Salopian who in due time was aided by Salopian endowments, I cannot but feel some sympathy with the local feeling of grievance.

The boarders were drawn from all parts of the Kingdom. There was a strong contingent from Wales, and another from Lancashire and the northern counties. For a year or more I was in Rigg's Hall, the small house of the Second Master. John Rigg himself came from Cumberland and spoke with a marked Cumbrian brogue. A little man with a big head, ever snapping his eyes and twitching his ears, no casual observer would have suspected him of power to win the respect of boys. But boys are generally sound judges of their pastors and masters, and I never knew a Rigg's Hall boy that had not a good word for this large-hearted kindly man. His team of about ten boarders were mostly good fellows, but there was at least one undesirable youth, an inheritance from the slack days of Rigg's predecessor. The want of Sixth Form boys was a drawback, but the Hall had a not unjustifiable self-esteem, and was conscious of being better fed than other school units. At the end of 1863 I left it for Doctor's Hall, the Headmaster's chief house, and was right in so doing; but I always felt attached to Rigg's.

The general conditions of life in the Halls were rough and simple; in fact almost medieval. The bedrooms, with from three to six in each room, were not amiss; but the washing and other appliances were out of date. Each boy had a little basin near his bed. For anything beyond this he had to make his way down to a paved chamber on the ground floor, in which cold water and zinc basins were to hand. There he could swill himself, or practise mutual swilling with a friend. Then up again to his room for a hasty dressing. In Doctor's Hall the water in the swill-room was got from a big leaden tank bearing a date of Charles II's time. In the winter months the process was trying, but young blood could stand it. In Jee's Hall, the Headmaster's second house, I believe the conditions were even more discouraging. Some other details may be better imagined than described. It all sounds hopelessly unsanitary, but in fact the health of the school in my time was remarkably good. Epidemics passed us by, and a good deal of the 'going out of school' on plea of sickness was notoriously shamming. Only once in five years did we break up prematurely, owing to the menace of scarlet fever, and this only a week before the end of the Half; and the infection did not spread. The year of three Terms was not introduced till Kennedy left. I think we may infer that our diet, though undeniably 'plain,' was not insufficient. We had to live on it for long continuous periods, for pocket-money soon failed as a means of supplement, and hampers from home were not so normal a relief

as they were at Dedham. We grumbled, of course:
but under Mrs Kennedy's management we did
pretty well. No rascally butler was (as happened
later) allowed free play to line his own pockets
by blackmailing tradesmen and robbing the commissariat.

Morning Chapel at 7 30 was a cheerless event,
but necessary; and First Lesson 8 to 9, usually
repetition of some sort, was endured somehow
under a cloud of hunger. Breakfast at 9. Second
Lesson 10 to 12 was the chief item in the day's
work. From 9 30 to 10 the Sixth Form boys carried
on a joint preparation, the Head Boy of Doctor's
translating the passage for the day to the rest, who
could and did make suggestions. On most days
more than half an hour was at disposal, as the
Doctor usually went up late to Top Schools, the
big room where he took the Sixth. We followed
him up: the day-boys would be there already.
Of the ever-varying phenomena experienced in the
course of these great lessons I have spoken above.
This I will not now repeat. Suffice it that we were
never bored. The Doctor threw himself into the
book before us with an intensity that kept dullness
at bay. To stand on the 'rostrum' and translate
under the glare of his eye was a severe ordeal for
a new hand. The needed nerve came by practice,
for you learnt to be calm when your blunders
caused him to explode, and he was soon all smiles
again. When the day's portion was got through,

he translated it himself in a vigorous impromptu style, without polish, but stimulating through its warmth and speed. Thus he carried his hearers with him and made them feel the voices of the Classics as those of living men.

From 12 to 2 we were free, but some of the lower form boys would be kept in by Detentions, as described above. Games and Sports in their several seasons claimed this interval. After dinner at 2 the day's order varied. Tuesday and Thursday were Short-lesson days, with school from 3 to 4. Monday Wednesday and Friday Long-lesson days, 3 to 5. Saturday was a Half-holiday. A record of Academic successes of Old Salopians was kept by the Head boy, and extra Half-holidays were claimed and granted on account of these according to a regular tariff. Beside this the Sixth often had their Monday afternoon free on the strength of the last week's exercises being good. This 'Sixth Extra' was the best working time in the week, for the other forms were safe in School. I once had the great honour of earning one of these Extras, owing to Kennedy's extravagant praise of a single exercise. Up jumped the Head Boy and made him grant it then and there. The rest of the day varied with the time of year. Tea (bread and infinitesimal butter, known as Boards,) came at 7, after which the lower boys had a spell of 'preparation' up in Top Schools. The Sixth worked in their common rooms and went up to prayers with the rest at 9. Bed-time was at 10. I must mention the custom of closing the day's lesson work by the prayer 'Lighten our darkness'....said by each master in his own class-room. It had a much more gracious effect than most religious formalities, coming at the end of third lesson in unrehearsed setting. In the case of the Doctor it sometimes would be the unbroken continuation of a final joke.

This leads me to make a few remarks on the religious side of the school life. The Chapel was an oblong room under the old Library, fitted up with benches, masters' desks, and pulpit, and a special desk for the praepostor on duty, who called over the names at the end of morning prayer, and acted as a sort of clerk. On Sundays the boarders attended St Mary's Church for morning service, and School Chapel in the afternoon. The latter function was a full service, with a sermon from the Headmaster. During my time some of the upper boys got leave to start a choir, and hymns were introduced. On the last Sunday of the Half it became the custom to sing 'Brief life is here our portion,' a mild con-cession to schoolboy humour. The movement led to the establishment of the School Concert as a yearly event, a most successful enterprise entirely due to boys' initiative. In the last two or three years of the Kennedy period there was in fact a marked rise in the religious tone of the school. This I attribute to the influence of a few boys who came from homes in which the Church revival on new

lines had begun to tell with effect. Some of these
were relatives of the Doctor. I do not propose to
discuss the thorny subject of Religion in Schools,
but to aim at a truthful picture of actual conditions.
Lessons in Divinity there were, of course. Of these
one may say in general that they served to promote
knowledge of the dogmas then in vogue. That these
had much direct influence on the school morality
I cannot venture to affirm. The light-hearted
acceptance of youth is apt to be coupled with a
faculty of easy dismissal; and a mechanically
orthodox system is not readily adapted by boys to
solve the daily problems of life. On the whole
school morals were good. In later years, when I
was brought into touch with men from other
famous schools, where religion was a more out-
standing item in the school programme, I was often
led to reflect on conditions at Shrewsbury. My
conclusion was that we had not suffered much
from the old-fashioned devotion to routine. The
plan of serving out rations of dogma, and leaving
it to sink in somehow, was not so bad as it might
seem to more modern enthusiasts. The well meant
effort, strong in some schools, to promote a rise
in religious temperature was (as observation shewed)
no real protection against moral collapse.

A most important element in our school life was
self-government in sports and games. The indifference, not to say dislike, with which Dr Butler
regarded this part of schoolboy interests, is well

known. Here Kennedy was a reformer. He secured a field for cricket and football on Coton Hill, less than a mile away. This, though not well suited to the purpose, was in full use. Football prospered more than cricket. The old Shrewsbury game was rather like that played at Harrow. But we played in the mass, and it was somewhat in the style of a Homeric battle, with the heroes rushing about in the heat of the fray, and the common herd striving to avoid entanglement in the collision of 'mighty opposites.' For football was compulsory by unwritten school-law, and all boarders, unless grudgingly exempted by doctor's orders, had to bear a part. 'Douling game' was formally announced by the Hall Crier at breakfast. The day of select teams was not come, but signs were appearing. The chief players were beginning to dress for the game, and the match Sixth *v* Schools was played both in the mass and by Elevens. Play was improved when a few of the leading dayboys began to be admitted, such as R Tomlins and A H Gilkes. After my time the school produced a champion player for Cambridge and for England, H Wace, a native of Shrewsbury. An institution on which we especially prided ourselves was the 'Runs' held in the months of autumn and early winter. It was modelled on the traditional lines of fox-hunting. There was a Huntsman, with Senior and Junior Whips. Runners of proved prowess were 'Gentlemen,' as were also the Sixth Form *ex officio*. These ran in suitable

clothes, and were expected to give an arm of help
to 'Hounds' that were in danger of dropping out of
the pack: a service not useless, for to fall out some
distance from home might have been a serious thing
to a small boy who did not know the country. The
Hounds had to run in their everyday clothes, with
a 'mortar-board' to wear or carry. The use of torn
paper for 'scent' did not mean that the course of
the Run varied according to the caprice of the two
Gentlemen who went as Foxes. Each of the eleven
Runs had its own traditional course, and scent was
at times omitted if for any reason there was need
of hurry to the start. An enterprising Huntsman
would sometimes invent a new Run in place of one
of the old ones. But he went over the ground first
himself, and such innovations were rare. It must
not be forgotten that authority looked askance at
the Runs, mainly because some of them took the
boys 'out of Bounds.' In short they were winked
at, not approved, and this made them all the more
popular. The possible evils of exhaustion were the
boys' own care. At tea after a Run each Hound
received a 'hot supper,' a dish of something meaty,
sent in from Mother Wade's, paid for out of a fund
subscribed by the Gentlemen. And in the 'Long,'
the chief event of the Season, only picked Hounds
chosen by the Huntsman were allowed to start.
Scratchley's Long (1866) was a severe experience,
not to be lightly forgotten.

The Runs are a delicious memory, but I refrain

from enlarging on the joy of dashing across country in the fulness of strength and spirits and in jolly company. The athletic sports known as May Races, and the Senior and Junior Steeplechases, were much what they are at other schools. But a curious custom, derived from the regular Turf, was observed. Each boy entered for any of these events was given the name of a horse and credited with an owner. The opportunity was used, sometimes in malice, to indicate slyly any peculiar quality or circumstance observed in individuals. Thus a notoriously greedy youth would be *Believer* (belly ever), a favourite of Fisher the mathematical master has been *Finikin* (finny kin), and so on. As a vent for a little passing spleen I do not think this practice did any harm, but the inner meaning of some names was not pretty. They were printed on a regular race card.

I pass now to the river, the Severn as it was and is no longer. Endless tricks of watermanship could be learnt in boating on that wayward stream. We learnt to row as best we might—by rowing. Coaching only began in 1864 when a yearly four-oar race with Cheltenham was arranged. And the master who undertook it was not competent in that department, while the Rev T Lloyd, an old Lady Margaret cox, was too busy in his parish. But, if the style of rowing was bad, the tackling of awkward fords and other hindrances was a training in handiness. There was no Boat Club with boats of its own, until

I got one started in the winter of 1866, which set to work in the season of 1867. T G Cree was my good comrade in the movement. The old plan was as follows. A Regatta Captain was elected by Doctor's Hall early in the year. He had to prepare a list of applicants for boating leave, which included leave to pass through the town on the way to the Quarry. He had to give the Headmaster assurance that to the best of his belief all those named on the list could swim. But there was no test, and a boy's own declaration was accepted, sometimes wrongly. I got a swimming-test enforced in 1867. The list passed, we proceeded to form crews of friends. Then each crew made its bargain with an old shark of a boat-owner for the hire of a four-oar for the season. We were swindled, of course. Some time in April we began rowing, and had about three good rowing days a week until the regatta in June. No uniforms were in use; they appeared only on regatta day. In the latter part of the season races were held between the crews to determine the order of starting for a bumping-race at the regatta. This last was a poor thing in itself, and much of its popularity was connected with 'Regatta Dinner,' an open-air feast under the trees on Shelton Rough. There in lovely surroundings we went through our performance with true schoolboy solemnity, made speeches and drank healths, in imitation of our elders,—and so home for Call-over and the bumping-race after tea.

Truth forbids me to dissemble the fact that cases of undue elation were liable to occur, we being unused to strong drink. The dinner in 1865 was rather a disaster. In 1866 Dr Kennedy was resigning, and wanted to take leave of us all at a great supper in the evening of regatta day. No doubt he had long been uneasy about our yearly festival, but had not seen his way to forbid it. He sent for me (then Regatta Captain) and said that in view of the farewell supper he must forbid the dinner. I knew what a disappointment this would cause, and entreated him to recall his decision. If he would trust me, I would see the affair through without scandal. The fine old man yielded to this piece of youthful assurance. And I carried out my bargain. My schoolfellows were, I knew, not to be impressed by 'jaw,' so I said nothing, but quietly secured the support of a few school leaders, and made success certain by providing only well diluted drinks. When I went a day or two after to take my own leave of my beloved Head, he thanked me for my service in his well-known style. Proud was I, and I record the incident here to shew that once upon a time I did a good thing and did it neatly.

Bathing was on a primitive footing. How far the School authorities took cognizance of it, I never ascertained. It was known to go on, and the presence of certain hangers-on, not regular school servants, one of whom attended on the river bank

at the bathing-place, implied recognition of some
kind. The place was not very suitable, but a better
was hardly to be found. The water at the upper
part was deep, at the lower shallow. There was no
instruction beyond what one boy might give to
another. The only case of accident I remember was
when some of us took an illicit dip out of the season,
and a big fellow got into danger. A smaller comrade
rescued him, and we kept the matter secret. This
illustrates what I said above as to the way in which
we were left free to conduct our own boyish affairs.
Accustomed to a republican system, holding elections of officers, and governed by our own traditional
rules, we were cool young hands. When Moss came
as Head, we that saw the change bitterly resented
his moves towards more official control. But the old
regime, dating from Butler, had to go.

Now for a word on Bounds. The site of the old
Schools may have been suited to the conditions of
the sixteenth or seventeenth century. By the time
of Butler's coming (1798) there were many drawbacks, some of which he managed to get removed.
An account of these may be found in Fisher's
Annals. But the only within-bounds exit to the
country, by way of Coton Hill, led in my time
through a street then of doubtful reputation and
abounding in public houses. I do not think that
much harm came of our necessary passage along
this route, and some of the houses were most
respectable. But things did happen now and then,

and I have seen one or two cases of boys in beer. Such cases were very rare and were getting rarer. The lure of the illicit shewed itself in a queer custom. As winter months passed by, there came a Sunday, known as Fox Sunday, when one of the afternoon Call-overs was dropped, having come too near the other. This meant that there was on that day a longer free space of time than on any other in the year. There was thus an opportunity for visiting the *Fox* inn at Albrighton out along the Chester road. By hard walking it was possible to do this and get back again for Call-over. As the vigorous tramp worked off the beer, no harm was done, and the spice of adventure commended the trip, even to some of the Sixth Form. What will not boys do to take a sporting risk? There was a tradition that in earlier days Munro had reached the race-course by hanging on to the buffer of a railway truck, and the story of how Marmaduke Lawson jumped over the railings erected by Dr Butler is on record.

Of many odd school details I say nothing—such as Merit Money—for they are set forth in Fisher's *Annals*. But a word as to certain queer characters who haunted the Schools and were a part of our surroundings. Ebrey was a cunning loafer of ill-defined duties. He attended the bathing-place in the summer, until I turned him off in favour of 'Cotton' (John Thomas), who looked after the playing-field and blew up the footballs, made with natural bladders, by the sheer force of his lung-power. I have seen him do it, not a pretty sight. He also performed services in connexion with the boats, and was on the whole a person of no small merit. Ireland was represented by old 'Pat,' who hung about School Gates ready to go on errands to shops that were out of bounds or do any small service in hope of reward. His gains must have been very small, and they were certainly invested in drink rather than in soap. During our holidays he resided in the workhouse. Poor old 'Sue' the half-crazy apple-woman sat by the gate and now and then found a customer. Old Lloyd, who had charge of the boot-room and neglected to clean the boots, was a character such as Sterne would have enjoyed. He had been a soldier, and his vocabulary suggested long service in Flanders.

One of the chief restraints on our general freedom was the lack of ready money. Few of us came from wealthy homes, and to raise funds for any common purpose was not easy. It is now I believe the custom at Schools to have a sort of sports-budget officially recognized, and to charge the total subscription in the school bills. We knew nothing of such arrangements. The captains of each sport or game fixed the several subscriptions, and they were collected with more punctuality than might have been expected. This meant that at certain times a captain or treasurer had in his hands a considerable sum in cash. In my last year I was for a time holding public moneys to an amount that fairly alarmed me. What if it were stolen from my locker in Headroom during the night? Yet I had no better place in which to keep it. It never occurred to me to ask one of the masters to take charge of it. So I held my tongue and trusted to Providence, and all ended well. Some of it was collected from benefactors outside for the boat-house that we were then hoping to build: this was eventually lodged in a bank, and has since been put to its intended use, but without recognition of those who collected it.

Another little matter deserves mention here. Call-over implied a School List. This the Praepostor of the week wrote out for himself. There was no official version. At length some enterprising youths had a list printed, and offered copies at a penny apiece not only to boys but to masters. The success of the speculation was so marked that the venture lasted out my time. Public opinion recognized a sort of equitable right to the monopoly, and the 'goodwill' was passed on to others. I remember once making a profit of 10/- on a single venture. Such was the origin of printed School Lists at Shrewsbury.

The departure of senior boys who were going to Oxford or Cambridge took place formerly in the middle of the Half; for they generally came back for a few weeks after the Midsummer holidays. On the Sunday before they left the Doctor preached his leaving sermon at afternoon chapel. The peroration would contain a reference to those bound for 'green fields and pastures new,' a misquotation of Milton that was apparently habitual. We used to go to the station to give the departing heroes a send-off, as no doubt our predecessors had done in the coaching days. The change to three Terms in the year put an end to this little bit of sentimental leave-taking. I do not know what was or is the case at other schools, but at Shrewsbury we took a keen interest in the doings of old boys in University life, beyond the events recorded in newspapers. I have still letters written to me while at school by friends at Cambridge, giving some vivid impressions of College life from within, and demanding School news in return. Undergraduates revisited their old School in June without restraint. This freedom was somewhat limited by Mr Moss—I believe, after consultation with other Headmasters. And it is true that the conversation of some young 'bloods' was a questionable enlargement of the schoolboy outlook. In these improved days perhaps no such restriction is necessary: I cannot tell.

To sum up my school experiences at Shrewsbury, first let me say that they fell in a period the like of which can hardly be seen again. Changes were urgently needed to enable the School to compete on an equal footing with other Schools of repute. There was no large endowment to bear the cost of such developments. Nor, it must be confessed, could they have been carried out on the historic site.

Sooner or later sentiment had to give way: meanwhile, both education and the details of daily life had to be kept going under immense difficulties. The one stable asset was reputation, and this consisted in the fame of Shrewsbury as a nursery of Classical scholars. Now in this respect Kennedy was well able to maintain, or even surpass, the standard attained under Butler. But against growing competition it was not possible for him to keep up the numbers and with them the income. Disguise it as we may, he was leading a forlorn hope for thirty years. That he was alive to the need of enlarging the school curriculum, is proved by his making Mathematics and French part of the regular work: and under Mr Paget it is evident that mathematical teaching was a success. But that was before my time, and Paget's mantle had not descended to his successor, who with many good qualities could neither keep order nor teach. French was rather a byword, and I can now see that the methods employed were a guarantee of failure. For Natural Sciences there was no provision at all. This was not the result of indifference on Kennedy's part. At one time he had been anxious to make a move in that direction. His daughters well remembered the stage at which his interest expressed itself in the use of a small chemical apparatus on his own account, and Samuel Butler bears witness to the fact in the *Way of all Flesh*. For Dr Skinner is Kennedy, drawn by a somewhat cruel hand.

A pitiful incompatibility clouded all the relations between Kennedy and his illustrious pupil. No fair judge will condemn the Doctor on S Butler's portrait of him, and they made up the difference in later years. And Dr Skinner is after all represented as a true gentleman, however led astray by a temperament that the future author of *Erewhon* could not understand. Kennedy was hasty, and his indignation was apt to explode without sufficient cause; but the reaction was superbly genial, if you only bided your time. I dwell on this point here because his impulsive nature shewed itself most fully in his generous treatment of others. It was this generosity that prevented him from weeding out the staff. He could not dismiss an inefficient master, and thus he added to the difficulty of improving the School. This task he bequeathed to his successor, who could not shirk it any longer. It was indeed a crying necessity that the School teaching should be improved throughout, and its credit not rest on the Sixth Form alone. But I have some reason to think that the old body of School Governors were content with things as they were. Some ten or fifteen years earlier, when the Doctor was minded to introduce Chemistry, they had not encouraged the design, whether from devotion to the Classics or on the plea of lack of funds for a costly venture. Anyhow such developments had to stand over until the removal of the School in 1882. For myself, looking back over a space of more than sixty years, and trying to estimate fairly what it is that I owe to Shrewsbury, I come to this conclusion. To Dr Kennedy I owe an awakening, not only in connexion with the study of the Classics, but through the stimulating influence of contact with a man of splendid talents, of a simplicity truly child-like, and extraordinary vigour. To the system, with its abundant freedom and openings for individual self-expression, I owe it that for better or worse I have all my life found it second nature to take an independent line, to support or oppose measures, not parties. This is not the way to 'succeed' in the world, but it breeds little remorse, and is a comfort in old age. To my old schoolfellows, most of whom have now departed this life, I owe all that comes of happy comradeship in the past and affectionate memories that will stay with me to the end.

I venture to add a few words on my experiences in dealing with the personal problem of transition from school to the University. Not that what concerns me individually is of any interest: but the questions that presented themselves to me may serve to illustrate the situation in which other youths have found themselves from time to time. From very early years I had taken note of the grown-up characters with whom I had been in contact, and the result of my observation had been a marked preference for Oxford types. My admiration of Dr Kennedy did not counteract this prejudice. No boy could help seeing that he was a quite exceptional person. And hitherto Cambridge had to me not been made attractive by the qualities of her representatives. But Shrewsbury was on the whole more in touch with Cambridge, and as time went by I gradually became conscious that my destiny led thither. One thing was certain; without very considerable aid from public endowments I could not hope to reach the University at all. Open entrance Scholarships at Colleges had recently been established, but even the best of these would not suffice to meet the needs of a boy whose parents, already embarrassed, could only contribute to his further maintenance by running further into debt. There remained the School Exhibitions, of which there were a good number. Most of these led to certain Colleges, but one or two were not so restricted. In particular, there were some charged on the general School funds, half of them leading to St John's College Cambridge, the other half quite free. It was important to find out what vacancies would occur in a given year. With the help of my steady old friend John Rigg I ascertained that 1866 would be a lean year, and 1867 a fat one. The date of my birthday made either year suitable for my leaving School. It was clear that I should have to wait till 1867, for the Exhibition vacant in 1866 was not likely to come my way. So I stayed on at the cost of another year's school expenses (more debts, in fact), and eventually secured a Minor Scholarship at St John's [£70 a year], a limited

School Exhibition [£50], and a further one [£35] also at St John's, on the Headmaster's nomination. With the help of a small balance of borrowed money I managed to get along until additional emoluments relieved my anxieties. These were, as may be imagined, a serious background of a young man's life; for I knew what a struggle my people were having to keep the home fires burning at Tenby. Moreover, I had not forgotten my failures at Winchester and Eton. I could not shake off a fear that in University competitions I should suffer the same crushing defeat. And by this time I fully understood that my business was to find some employment carrying immediate pay, that I might contribute to the expense of the education into which I had drifted by the force of circumstances.

APPENDIX TO SHREWSBURY CHAPTER

I print the following verses as an exceptional illustration of the sort of thing that went on at Shrewsbury during the Sixth Form mathematical lesson—10 to 12 on Saturdays. The author was R D Hodgson (afterwards Archer-Hind) who was known in Cambridge later on as Fellow and Lecturer of Trinity. I think the date of the lines would be the latter part of 1865, when Hodgson was only 17 or younger. Dr Kennedy had recently omitted to take a lesson owing to an attack of bronchitis. But it was known that he had celebrated his birthday on the preceding day. This gave occasion to R D H's poem written in pure mischief to relieve the dullness of two utterly futile hours.

BENJAMIN'S FEAST—À LA DRYDEN

I

The sun had shot his dying glance o'er Severn's
    troubled wave,
And nature's voice was silent with the silence of
    the grave:
The gloomy heaven above it gave a duskly lurid
    glare,
And the fitful breeze moaned sadly like a lost soul's
    last despair.
        And Salop's ancient piles
          Loomed dimly to the sight:
        Within were mirth and smiles,
          Without—the stormy night.
            Within were joy and gladness,
            Without were gloom and sadness:
Without were clouds and storm, within a hall with
    feast bedight.

II

For here a joyful company—'twas sure a goodly
    sight!
Had met to keep the happy day when Ben first
    saw the light,
And revelry and laughter made the walls resound
    again;
The mirth grew loud, the bottle passed, in honour
    of our Ben.
        And he, the ancient hero,
          Feasted right manfully;

And sorrow was at zero,
  Joy at infinity,
    And every beam and rafter
    Trembled with songs and laughter,
And ne'er a thought of ill was there to mar the
  festive glee.

III

But ah! swift-fated mortals nought possess without
  alloy:
Their day is turned to darkness, sorrow follows
  after joy:
Winter follows summer—headache follows too much
  wine,
And Ben, alas, for feasting pays the retributive fine.
    For the sun's morning glory
      Finds him in wretched plight:
    Bronchitis was the story,
      Sickness the truth and right.
      O rising generation,
      Be advised by this narration;
You'll have headache in the morning if you take
  too much at night.

CAMBRIDGE

I came into residence at Cambridge in October
1867, and found my footing through the welcome
of old schoolfellows in many Colleges. One soon
felt at home in conditions of more liberty, but was
conscious of a certain fall. Two years of increasing
authority and responsibility at School had left their
mark, and it seemed strange that the removal of
accustomed restraints should coincide with a sense
of insignificance. This feeling died away, and I was

content to be a mere Freshman, led by the upper years. But I did not easily lose my wonder at the clumsy mismanagement of their own affairs by Undergraduates. A Freshman was naturally interested in the details of Sports and Games, and the organization and finance of these was in those days very different, very inferior to what it is now. Clubs were generally in debt, and the senior men responsible for that situation took their Degrees and went down, leaving their successors to 'carry on' under a troublesome burden. Delayed payments meant higher charges: a boat club in debt to the boatbuilder could not well employ another tradesman, and so on. The universal credit system meant high prices at the shops. In short, everything seemed to rest on a supposition that everybody must and would incur liabilities to be met some day by excessive payments. And I believe that cases of ultimate default were very rare. A tradesman of high standing once said to me 'Oh yes, the Gentlemen always pay in the end.' College Kitchens were a standing provocation to extravagance. They were I think all leased to speculators, who made their profit out of undergraduate luxury. Thus they compensated themselves for having to provide dinner in Hall at a low contract price. Their position was a strong one, and it was not easy for College authorities to check the growth of an Undergraduate's Kitchen bill, or indeed to exercise any pressure on the College Cook. It is only right to add that Owen Jones the Johnian Cook died a poor man. In such an economic atmosphere as this no wonder College servants were tempted to plunder their masters. I had early experience of this. When I reached Cambridge, dinner in Hall was over for that day, and I was hungry. The gyp offered to fetch me something from the Kitchen, and suggested a cold fowl. I knew that at Tenby a fowl was cheap enough, so I consented, having in prospect several meals at no great cost. I made a sparing meal, leaving at least three quarters of the bird. Next morning the gyp called me and asked whether he should order me a breakfast from the Kitchen. I answered No, and he went off. On entering my keeping-room, I saw only 'Commons' on the table—that is, bread and butter. I searched the gyp-room; but there was no cold fowl, so I breakfasted without it. On the gyp's return, I asked what had become of it. He replied with easy assurance that the Gentlemen always left the remainders of dishes to their gyps. I thanked him for his care of my social proprieties, adding that I would consult my Tutor on the matter. He at once deprecated troubling a busy official with so trivial an issue, and generously offered to waive his own rights in the future for my benefit. So I held my ground; but he ate that fowl, and the Cook charged it to me at the peculiar College price.

The ordinary Undergraduate took little interest in the Dons outside those of his own College, whom

he regarded on the ground of their several qualities
with respect indifference amusement or contempt.
Of the Johnians I will speak below. It was owing
to an old schoolfellow, who had an appetite for
personalities and studied his surroundings, that I
came to know by sight a number of notable figures
of the old generation then passing away. Of College
Heads there were some fine old specimens, such as
Ainslie of Pembroke [elected in 1828], Archdall-
Gratwicke of Emmanuel [elected 1835, had served
at Waterloo], Cookson of Peterhouse [elected 1847].
Such venerable ancients aroused my fresh curiosity,
and I was at a loss to imagine what they found to
do. Whewell had died in 1866, and W H Thompson
ruled in Trinity. The Greek Professorship vacated
by him had now passed to Kennedy, so my old
Headmaster came into residence and was for more
than twenty years a noted Cambridge character.
I once, and once only, saw Adam Sedgwick, who
had been chosen Professor of Geology in 1818 and
lived till 1873. Stories of various kinds were told
of the Heads of Jesus [Corrie], Sidney [Phelps],
Queens' [Phillips], Caius [Guest], but I fancy I
did not hear these until later. The St Catharine's
affair was still fresh in gossip, though six years old.
More stories got through to Undergraduates than
the Dons suspected, and perhaps do still. An
amazing credulity, combined with youthful gift of
colouring, generally marked these traditions; which,
in days when there were far fewer sporting events

to chatter about, helped to give variety to conversation. A good specimen, but of later date, is the case of an altar-cross in gold presented to a certain College Chapel by the Master's wife. It was well known that the happy pair had waited many years before venturing on marriage. It was said that the lady's engagement-ring was included in the material of the cross. But the full undergraduate story was that the sacred object was made out of her engagement-rings.

SOCIAL MATTERS AND SPORTS

One significant difference in College life then and now strikes me forcibly as I look back on the past. Social distinctions created by wealth and poverty, or by family position and traditions, were still recognized with some frankness. This was not mere snobbery; the toadyism of Dons courting the favour of young noblemen, common enough in the eighteenth century, was no longer an undisguised feature of Academic life. But levelling views were not as yet dominant. Noblemen and Fellow-Commoners, though few, were a class in being, with distinctive Academic dress. I remember several cases in various Colleges, habited in various robes of silk and gold with sometimes a touch of velvet. In Trinity they wore blue and silver, and you might see a group of them if you happened to go into the great court in the morning. A few Fellow-Com-

moners were men above the usual age of Undergraduates, but the majority were quite young.
Their privileges (and fees) were higher than those
of the ordinary Pensioners. Probably some of them
thought their position a bore; indeed it was out
of date, and in a few years' time it was abolished,
Trinity leading the way. Below the general mass
of Pensioners came the class of Sizars. These also,
though their position was only a College fact, were
recognized by the University, and their status
carried with it a lower scale of fees. But they were
no longer the humble dependants of patrons. A few
Sizarships were still given by nomination, but in
general some examination-test governed the award.
A candidate had of course to profess poverty, but
the real guarantee of need lay in willingness to
accept such marks of inferiority as dining at a
separate table in Hall. The percentage of Sizars
was largest at St John's, and their abilities and
industry accounted for many of the Honours gained
by Johnians in University class-lists. The best of
them became Scholars and Fellows. The institution
worked as a means by which a clever youth could
rise in the world, provided he and his relatives
would 'stoop to conquer.' There was however a
disadvantage in having a large number of them.
They could not all be of first-rate ability. The more
there were of them, the more risk there was of their
being treated as a social class, a result to which
British snobbery only too easily tends. And the

Sizars of inferior quality were no great acquisition. There was unfortunately a temptation to use a Sizarship as a step in an ecclesiastical career. A Cambridge Degree was an asset to a curate. Now abolition of religious Tests did not come till 1871, and we were all assumed to be members of the Established Church. The Dons in power lost no chance of promoting what they conceived to be Church interests. At St John's one form of this policy was laxity in election of Sizars. Of this I have no doubt. It had been going on for some time: a passage in the *Way of all Flesh* shews that S Butler had already noticed it. And the open Scholarships at nearly all Colleges were beginning to draw off some of the pick of those who used to be content with Sizarships: hence the latter were ceasing to serve their better purpose. At Trinity, Sizarships were fewer and much more valuable.

All these institutions, and the social distinctions that went with them, have now practically disappeared; that is, so far as legislative changes can abolish them. Names remain, but no longer imply the same conditions. The causes and effects of the levelling movement that has put all Undergraduates on virtually the same footing, are I think not always clearly estimated. The Liberalism of the nineteenth century was to a great extent the voice of the poorer Middle Class, whose political and social appetite had been whetted by the triumph of the first Reform Bill. The old Universities were particularly exposed to attack. They had become the exclusive seats of aristocratic privilege and Church monopoly; they were no longer active leaders of the thought of the age. And this at a time when the House of Lords had been forced to bow to the popular clamour, and the Church, long given up to timeserving and quest of 'preferment,' had not yet been fully roused from lethargy to life. The pressure on Oxford and Cambridge came from a combination of two distinct forces. The Dissenters, characteristically vocal, demanded the abolition of Tests, joining hands with Radicals of all sorts, to whom the destruction of every trace of privilege was an end in itself. The operative causes must be recognized as having been negative in character. The effects of this levelling policy have not been equally negative. When it comes to levelling, the leveller wants to level some other class down, but would gladly level his own class up. The Liberal parent may be willing that his son's education should be less costly through the tenure of a Sizarship; but he will resent anything that may seem to mark an inferior status. Now to combine the receipt of charity with a defiant assertion of equality of status is pardonable as an aspiration, but as a gesture it is not of high moral value.

These survivals and changes are not without importance in a retrospective view. Side by side with these official statutory facts are others of a purely unofficial nature. Rightly or wrongly, the status of

a Sizar did connote a certain inferiority in the undergraduate world. That this was so may be illustrated
by reference to the customary law or practice of
some College boat-clubs. Of three such clubs
existing in Trinity one ['Second Trinity'] was
known to admit Sizars, and said to have been
originally founded for their accommodation. It had
a great tradition of old victories behind it, and
contained a number of members who rose to distinction in later life. It had in 1867 still several
years to run before it was dissolved as no longer
needed. But the segregation of the poorer and less
fashionable men, Sizars and others, was a significant
survival of social ideas that were already dying. In
St John's, the Lady Margaret club claimed to be
select, admitting members by ballot. A rival club,
the Lady Somerset, was recently extinct, after a
few years of life: but I have seen its ribbon worn
on a club straw. Another venture of the same kind
was started later, and had the same fate. I do not
think that the Lady Margaret ever excluded any
class of men as a class. But the black-ball, when
used, operated to the same effect. The present
system of one large club including all sport and
game interests—the 'Amalgamation'—dates only
from 1886, and was to my knowledge only possible
after a supreme effort to pay off the Lady Margaret
debt and start clear. These details may seem trivial,
but in truth are not so. It is to be remembered that
the Purchase-system was only abolished in the

British army as a consequence of the alarm caused by the events of the Franco-German war of 1870-1. Efficiency was seen at last to be a sheer necessity, and the influence of rank and wealth received a severe shock. The forward movement of public opinion was not without effect even in the University.

A curious affair of the time illustrates what I have just said. Oxford had been winning the Boat race year after year, and an improvement in Cambridge rowing was generally desired. This eventually took place under the kind direction of G Morrison, a famous Dark Blue oarsman, carried out by the splendid work of J H D Goldie. But meanwhile there were those who thought that, if the noble art was to be kept alive after revival, Cambridge should be more regularly represented at Henley Regatta, then dominated by Oxford crews. It was urged that College crews could not be relied upon to keep up the steady succession of competitors, and the revived tradition would die out. So it was proposed to establish a club for the special purpose of sending at least one good boat to Henley in each year. To make it fashionable, its membership was to be confined to those who came from certain schools. A fair number of men joined it, and some even paid their subscriptions. I remember noticing at the time that the oarsman chosen for captain of the projected boat, though a sportsman of remarkable skill, came from a school not included in the list. Well, the boat went to Henley, but was not exactly a success. Before the October Term began the club had somehow vanished, and not a soul was wearing their ribbon. How its debts were discharged I never learnt. Since those days many a College crew has competed at Henley and many victories have been won. I do not think that an enterprise such as that I refer to above would find favour nowadays.

I cannot resist the temptation to recall a few events of the time in the rowing world. It was the period of painstaking and revival, for men were sick of the long series of Oxford victories, and bent on the removal of Cambridge defects. Of the leading College clubs it was felt that First Trinity was too pedantic, and Third Trinity too reckless, as schools of oarsmen. Some thought that the choice of men for the University boat was corrupted by bias in favour of one or other of these styles. When Emmanuel won the Fours in 1867, this view was strengthened. When Sidney did the same in 1868 and 1869, it was confirmed. The May Races of 1868 were significant. Among the upper boats, Third Trinity looked to bumping First, despising the rather weedy Lady Margaret behind them. LMBC were in their turn menaced by Trinity Hall. In those days the distances between the boats were less than now, the course ended at the railway bridge, and there were six nights of racing. Furious spurts, and bumps made at Grassy Corner, were the order of the day. If a boat got away clear from the rush at Grassy, it might hope to escape later on. For the mad dash of the chasing boat led to excessive rudder-work in rounding the bend, and time thus lost was not easily regained. Under these conditions, First Trinity by strength were just able to foil Third. Lady Margaret, stroked by a man of singular coolness and skill, kept away from the Hall, a much more powerful crew. Such racing as this was a sight not to be forgotten. On the fifth night a great surprise came. Third Trinity, to better their chances, took in a new man at 5, and the venture failed. LMBC not only kept away from their pursuers but caught the exhausted Third late in the course. Nor did the restoration of their former 5 enable Third to recover their place on the last night. Skilled watermanship in the person of A J Finch, stroke of LMBC, had triumphed. In 1869 the distances between boats were lengthened, but the course was not, owing to the piles of the old railway bridge. This enabled First Trinity to remain Head of the River for three more years.

But to anyone who cared for rowing as an art there were in those races other phenomena of interest. I well remember noting the descent of Pembroke night after night, the penalty of trying to make a boat go by mere strength: they were a magnificent lot of men, but not a crew. Another curious fact was the rise of Emmanuel, also 'beefy' but better together. Still more striking was it to observe that, while Emmanuel closed up on the first group of boats, and caught Trinity Hall on the last night, Christ's were gaining on them. Any unbiassed critic could see that there was fine material for revival of the best of sports. Lower down too there were points not unworthy of notice. Magdalene, a sickly crew, not able to stand hard training, made more bumps than any other boat. They were perfectly 'together,' and their boat fitted them well and travelled with an ease that I have never seen equalled. In the language of Biology they were a 'sport.' Jesus were just beginning to creep up, destined soon to be Head of the river and to stay there for many years. I am not writing the history of Cambridge rowing, so here I stop. What I have said may be interesting as a record of a set of conditions just before the great revival began.

A quaint figure down river was old B Jolley the ferryman, known as 'Charon.' Most men who went down to the races walked along the towpath and crossed to the Chesterton side just below the 'Pike and Eel' in his boat, a regular fen-pattern punt, seldom upset in the hustle, but often nearly so. His tombstone in Chesterton churchyard records his fame.

Besides rowing, the undergraduate diversions included Cricket and the Athletic Sports, and not much else. Cricket, already tending to specialization and employing Professionals, was in practice

rather expensive, the game of a few. Football was
not much in favour, regarded then as rather a boys'
game. Riding was common enough, of course
among those who could afford it. The quiet reading
men mostly took their exercise on foot, and often
went long walks in the country. A grave hindrance
to long walks on Sundays was the rule then in force
of having to wear Cap and Gown—a hateful
burden. These walks meant close companionship
and exchange of views, and were in truth a valuable
part of the varied processes that made up an
University training. Two friends met mind to mind,
not in the presence of others, as at a club meeting.
But for non-reading men (who were many in those
days) there were not enough harmless amusements.
Long walks they generally despised: the exercise
was too humdrum to suit youths with no ideas to
exchange and prone to intellectual rest. Not a
few went to the bad; far more, I fancy, than do
nowadays. It is not easy for an old resident to
reach a sound conclusion on such a point. I can
only judge from what I happen occasionally to
hear, and from the general bearing of the young
Barbarians in the courts and streets. The change
in respect of dress is very marked. I never now see
the downright dressy man, such as one constantly
met in the old days; and a very good thing too.
Entertaining, if I am rightly informed, is also not
what it was in my time. A favourite meal was breakfast, a most elaborate affair, at which sometimes as

many as ten or a dozen undergraduates would sit down to a copious spread. Beginning at 9, they would not break up till 11 or later. Cups of various kinds and strength, from cider and claret to ale and 'copas,' passed round after the duty of eating was solemnly discharged, and tobacco and lively talk conducted the party to an end. Another social function was performed in the 'Wines' after Hall, a self-conscious imitation of the usages of grown-up people, in truth very foolish, and liable to abuse. But we knew that the Dons entertained each other thus, and some of them invited Undergraduates to wine. In some Colleges it was a regular custom for the Second Year to join forces and give three or four big Wines to the Freshmen in the October Term. These conventional wine-bibbings led to much indiscretion. I believe these extravagant scenes of eating and drinking are now long out of fashion. But a modern Undergraduate could speak with more authority on the point. My own impression is briefly this. Neither the luxury of the rich (or of those who followed their example), nor the penurious habits of the conscientious poor, are now in evidence as they were fifty or sixty years ago. There is on the whole less extravagance and less painful thrift. That the average expenditure of a student has fallen or risen, is to me doubtful Clubs have multiplied, and they are directly or indirectly a cause of expense. Entertainments are now largely joint affairs, such as College concerts

and balls: but some at least of these are lavish
enough. And new diversions are often of a costly
kind. When the student in his motor runs you
down in the public street, he is taking a liberty
denied to the poor. You may, if it please you, take
comfort from the thought that Mr Jehu Petrol is
probably sober.

For one accident of life the old conditions of
residence made no provision. If a man fell seriously
ill, there was no isolated sick-room to which he
could be sent for nursing: nor were trained nurses
within reach ready for such duty. He was treated
and attended in his rooms. If his disease were in-
fectious, visits were forbidden, but there was nobody
to enforce the order. So far as I know this state
of things was general. In St John's I have known
a man have scarlet fever, and yet be freely visited
by friends (I was one) in the peeling stage. Luckily
no one took the infection. When I was a B A, I
heard one evening that an Old Salopian at Corpus
had just broken his leg at football. I went off to
see him. He lay in bed in his keeping-room, which
it was not easy to enter. His friends were in such
force that there was hardly standing room for one
more. All were smoking hard, and a thick cloud
from twenty or more pipes and cigars made the
atmosphere choking and obscure. A sly hint that
this air might not be quite the best thing for the
patient, who could not leave his bed, evidently
opened a consideration that had not occurred to

the company. This is a good instance of the general blindness of young men to the claims of others. For the most part they mean no harm by this indifference, and only the coarser minority carry this social defect into later life. When some tall undergraduate bumps me off the pavement just as a motor draws near, I dislike the risk incurred through his impact, but I comfort myself by reflecting that he means no harm. He regards me as unimportant, and that is all. I am only thankful that such collisions are rare: the majority of men are considerate enough. But as each year goes down another comes up, and there is never lacking a 'supply of fit persons' to keep in being the traffic uncertainties of Cambridge streets.

That there might be a tragic side to the lack of means for dealing with sickness was brought home to me later when I was a College Tutor. One wet and gloomy evening I came upon one of my men just going out of College to fetch a doctor for a sick friend. He was himself very delicate, quite unfit to be out in such weather. Of course I sent him back to his rooms and did the errand. But the affair made me uneasy, and with reason: the poor lad, careless of his own welfare, died at home not long after. I trust that, what with nursing homes and a staff of trained nurses, patients and the doctors who treat them nowadays get a better chance. While on this topic, let me record the sympathetic kindness of the men in St John's New

Court in 1893, when I lay many weeks to all appearance dying of typhoid fever. When the skill of Doctor Bradbury and the devotion of my nurses pulled me through, I learnt of the self-imposed silence that had reigned around. Nay more, three brothers who kept in the large rooms above me, all devoted to music, hushed their beloved instruments till I recovered. This was a painful sacrifice, of which they generously made light. But it is not for me to forget the kindness of all, not only the Blackman brothers,—and I do not forget it.

In the years round about 1890 there were severe epidemics of Influenza. Cases were sometimes so numerous in College that no nurses could be found for most of them. Tutorial duty largely resolved itself into keeping an eye on the sick and seeing to the execution of doctors' orders. Gyps and bedmakers had a hard time of it. Fortunately we had no deaths. But one had to be up late, seeing that things were made snug for the night. Once or twice I had to take a share of nightly watching, when neither nurse nor relatives of the patient were available in a bad case. Good undergraduates helped in this duty. We may be thankful even in these days that such emergencies seldom arise.

THE VOLUNTEERS

I had almost forgotten the Rifle Volunteers, an omission not to be excused. The uneasiness as to the secret intentions of the French Emperor had set Rifle Corps going all over the country in the fifties and sixties of last century. Well meant, but doomed to inefficiency as a force, owing to the apathy of governments, these units survived as Rifle Clubs. There was some good shooting, but no organization to fit them for service in war. The CURV consisted of six companies, A to F, of which B was Johnian. No company was at full number in my time, and some were very thin. The enthusiasm of earlier days had died down, recruits were few, and it seemed unsatisfactory to have to pay a subscription for the honour of serving. So the 'bugshooters,' as they were called, did not stand high in undergraduate esteem. A few men of note joined, and managed to keep things going, but the majority were such as had no prospect of athletic distinction, and rather reminded one of the saying that it takes all sorts to make a world. The war of 1870–1 gave a little fillip to the corps. I joined with two others in the Long Vacation of 1870. We three were drilled in the Backs by Sergeant Garvin V C, a fine Irish soldier of the Mutiny days. We learnt to handle rifles, and to form Fours with imaginary comrades, until we passed muster so far as to be allowed to shoot on the range. This stage reached, we 'shot our classes' at the shorter ranges first, and then at the longer. Drills there were, but attendance was very irregular, and it took much pressure to make the average warrior qualify as 'efficient' by keeping

the required minimum. By the by, in 1871 Ensign
A P Humphry of Trinity won the Queen's Prize at
Wimbledon.

The uniform was a dull-coloured tunic knicker-
bockers and cap, tolerable if it fitted well. Needful
economy drove me to do as many did, buying a
second-hand suit. Alas, it had been made for some
lanky narrow-chested youth, and pinched me sadly
while it was no comfort to feel that I was making
a guy of myself in order to keep up the price of
Consols. The rifles were old Enfields, too much
worn to be retained by the regular army. There
was a risk that, when you had got the charge of
powder down, and then rammed down the bullet
in its greasy case, the bullet might slip back towards
the muzzle owing to the worn-out smoothness of
the barrel. So we were warned on the range never
to hold the loaded piece muzzle downward, for fear
of bursting it when fired. It was the custom to snap
a cap on your rifle before loading, and little pits
were provided into which this could be done. Jokes
about firing away your ramrod were of course not
out of date.

But in 1872 (I think) breech-loaders were served
out even at Cambridge. Inspection of the whole
battalion in the May Term quickly followed. I had
never handled a Snider breech-loader (converted
Enfield), when I was called to muster on the
Johnian lawn. In the struggle with my uniform
my cartridge-pouch slipped off my belt, and I was

hurried away without it. On the parade ground a number of blank cartridges was served out to me, and a Snider rifle. Having no pouch, I slipped the cartridges loose into my knickerbocker pocket. But the former owner had worn a big hole in the pocket, so the cartridges (each with its percussion cap) were assembled round my knee to my grave discomfort and possible risk. Inspection began, and I took part in a series of movements wholly new to me, following my neighbours' example as best I might. At the order to fire I imitated their gestures, but my cartridges were out of reach. Inspection done, we formed a square round the gallant General inspecting. He buttered up our performance, as he was bound to do, and hinted that he had never seen anything quite like it. But I am sure that he would have seen something very unlike it, if he had called on us to do it over again. What became of those cartridges that night in College I will not reveal, but the fact of their containing powder was in evidence. Such were the possibilities of Academic militarism in the golden days of old. I venture to offer my best wishes and admiration to the Officers' Training Corps, the reality of a generation strenuous and awake.

Let me record a curious little side-light on undergraduate life in the summer of 1870. Some reading-man up for work in the Long Vacation came across a wandering German in Cambridge, and found

his conversation (for he spoke English well) interesting. Visits to rooms in College followed, and not
a few students were ready to welcome a man from
the seat of war. He was a North German employed
in the commissariat service, short sight disquali-
fying him for the fighting line. On mobilization he
had to give up his post on the staff of a Berlin
newspaper, and feared that he would not be re-
instated on the return of peace. The French railways
were just beginning to be utilized for German
transport, and some of the commissariat corps were
given furlough for the time. So Förster came over
to England in hope of finding employment here.
This hope came to nothing, but undergraduate
hospitality relieved his passing necessities, and
probably increased the poor fellow's disappointment. Sympathy he did not lack, for at the moment
there was a general impression that the French
were in the wrong and their punishment served
them right. We youths listened eagerly to his stories.
I remember in particular how he insisted on the
unpleasantness of his own branch of the service.
Their waggon-trains were constantly 'sniped' by
Franc-tireurs, and their own defective sight prevented an adequate reply. In truth the position was
not an enviable one. At the last he was hard put
to it to find enough money to get back to Germany.
So he offered for sale all the little properties he
had about him, and we made such a market as
we could afford. Who bought his grandmother's

bible I forget: my share was a magnificent cane with a copper head. This I kept for some years, and lost by leaving it in a London cab.

RESIDENCE AND TEACHING

I must not forget to point out that Terms were kept by shorter residence than they are since 1882. In my time we had to keep two thirds of the days. Not long before this, one half only had been required. Arrangements of every kind were of course governed by the shortness of time at disposal. It is only necessary to consider this situation further so far as it affected matters of teaching. In general it may fairly be said that conscientious Lecturers suffered from want of room. To compress a serious course into six weeks or a trifle over was not always easy, and the temptation to slovenly haste was sometimes imperfectly overcome. But I had better speak in detail, first of Poll Lectures, then of Honour Lectures, and last of Private Tuition. Of Professorial Lectures little notice need be taken, as they did not give preparation for Examinations, and it was only to prepare for Examinations that men would go to lecture of their own accord. For certain purposes, that is to secure certificates of attendance, some Professorial courses had to be 'kept.' These were chiefly in the department of Divinity, and the compulsion was exercised by the Bishops, who made such certificates a condition of ordination. A student was expected to leave one of his cards as a record of attendance, and queer stories were told of the number of cards exceeding the number of students present. That men sometimes did leave a card for an absent friend may or may not be true: it was certainly believed. And, in any case, attendance and attention did not mean the same thing.

As to Poll lectures, it must be borne in mind that the examination-standard for the Ordinary Degree was scandalously low. Any lad of moderate intelligence who had been at a good school could very well have got up the subjects by himself,—that is, if he would only make the necessary effort; and I believe a few did so. But the mass of Poll men fell into two classes: first, those who scorned to do any work until an examination was close at hand, and then did everything hastily in the most unintelligent manner possible: secondly, those who were really stupid and only capable of being spoon-fed. Neither class could profit by lectures in which subjects were taken Term after Term in regular succession. The former declined a slow and regular procedure, evaded lectures in October, and 'crammed' in May. The latter needed to be drynursed all the time, if they were to get an unmerited Degree through the indulgence of examiners. The result was that while Lecturers were being paid for ineffectual work, private Coaches with a reputation for 'getting men through' throve on the constant

demand for their services. Hamblin Smith of Caius
was notable as being not only a successful Coach
but a real teacher, and a man respected by all.
I do not affirm that no men attained the Ordinary
Degree through the use of their College lectures.
Some few such there were, but mostly men who
could have done without any help beyond asking
an occasional question of a friend. Circumstances
differed in the several Colleges. Trinity only admitted students who could pass an Entrance examination, and by this means avoided a tiresome
and unnecessary problem. I believe that the most
complete provision (on paper) for Poll teaching
was that at St John's. It was a wasteful failure.

While the Poll Degree was no credit to the University, and the care of Poll men shamefully neglected,
in the case of Degrees with Honours a competition
of the crudest character prevailed. The so-called
Order of Merit existed in all Triposes. Merit meant
the relative number of marks gained by the several
candidates on a particular set of papers at a given
date. Marks were added together, and places in the
list determined by the totals. That the results thus
reached were infallibly correct, it was almost high
treason to doubt. And probably they were infallible so far as human fallibility allowed. Vast
pains were taken by examiners, and Cambridge
men regarded their rigid system with pardonable
self-satisfaction as the best thing of the kind in the
world. To be Senior Wrangler was the very crown

of Academic distinctions. Now, so long as you understood by 'merit' no more than I have stated above, there was no harm done. The fact of a man's place was indisputable. Error began when the fact of a given moment was regarded as fixing a man's intellectual place in the world for life. This absurdity was a manifestation of the 'sporting instinct' of which English people are grotesquely proud. Bets and sweepstakes were not wholly unknown, and Cambridge swarmed with men able to tell you the several years and places of all notable persons and of many obscure. The *Calendar*, unofficial though it then was, was often referred to as the Cambridge Bible, and the story ran that the last words of a respected College Head were 'give me a *Calendar*.' In the town, Tripos Lists were as interesting as news from Newmarket or Epsom. On going to order my B A gown and hood, my tailor made me a bow, pointed to our list posted up in the shop, and said in a voice of triumph 'we've got three in the first six, Sir.'

This state of things in examinations necessarily reacted on teaching. Your place was everything, and it had to be the highest possible: whether the means used to that end were the best training for you as a man or even as a scholar, was to most men irrelevant. It should be said that in Trinity this view was not generally accepted, and here and there signs of dissatisfaction were beginning to appear in other Colleges. In St John's our lecturers

were men with high Degrees and some of them
deeply learned. But somehow we did not seem to
profit much by their instruction. Mathematical and
Classical students agreed in the feeling that we did
not get what we wanted. Avoiding detailed criticism
of good men, I will only say that in my opinion the
ruling fault of a brilliant staff was that they did not
study their pupils personally so as to diagnose
individual cases. Even the set lectures to full class-
rooms were apt to be a blend of what men either
knew already or did not want to know at all.
Graves was an exception; no one wanted to 'cut'
his lectures, and Mathematical men spoke well of
Horne, if he were out of bed in time for an 8 o'clock
lecture. Those Classical lecturers who took the
small Composition classes were generally content
with exposing grammatical blunders and giving
you a 'fair copy.' To study the weaknesses that
were at the back of your inadequate versions (not
mere 'howlers'), and apply a suitable tonic treatment, was outside their range. To get any effective
individual instruction it was (or was thought) necessary to read with a Coach. A Coach would at any
rate not forget that you were reading for a Tripos,
and your success would be his single aim. Accordingly, some men had a Coach every Term, and
the Long Vacation as well. Those who hoped just
to squeeze into a First Class often did so, but I
think seldom with success. They did not do enough
private reading to profit by so much private

teaching—'tips' were all very well in their way, but they were not enough. I was, perhaps fortunately, not able to afford a regular Coach (at £9 a Term and 10 guineas for the Long,) and read much by myself. But I had some coaching, one Term indeed with Shilleto, at that time the leading Classical teacher.

It may be not wholly uninteresting to describe the proceedings in his study at No 1 Scrope Terrace, for it may safely be said that we shall not see their like again. My experience was perhaps somewhat abnormally grotesque, for I could only get an evening hour, the last of his long laborious day. For many years he had led a most exhausting life, coaching single pupils from 9 a m to 8 or 9 p m, with short intervals for meals. His habits had told upon an originally tough constitution, and he looked older than his real age. He did not smoke, but took snuff freely. Several snuff-boxes were about the room, presents from old pupils, but he could never lay his hand on them when wanted, so generally drew his pinch from a large tinfoil packet that stood in the middle of the table. On each such occasion he needed a handkerchief, and that speedily. It was somewhere on the floor, among the books with which the whole room was littered. In the search for it he was apt to catch his foot in a book, and sneeze prematurely; I have known him get an awkward fall in the attempt. Found and used, the handkerchief was dropped on the floor again in the line of traffic as he wandered to and fro. It was understood that during the day he drank a quantity of tea: at night, when I saw him, a pint pot of beer stood handy on a pedestal. When it was low ebb in this vessel, he placed it in a pigeon-hole close to the door, and rang the bell. Soon a stealthy hand withdrew it and put it back refilled. So much liquid refreshment entailed other embarrassing phenomena. Among these various doings the work went on. Criticism of an exercise consisted chiefly in telling you what you had done wrong and what you had better have written; that is, what would have been sound Latin or Greek according to the usages of the language (particularly Greek) recognized by scholars. He spoke with authority, and the outpouring of references (by chapter section or line), without opening a book, simply took your breath away. If you turned them out afterwards, lo they were correct. Truly an astounding feat of memory. In his own kind he was unrivalled, and other teachers bowed before the first Greek scholar in England. But whether it would have been well to enjoy a great deal of this instruction may be doubted.

Shilleto was in Holy Orders, though not essentially a Divine. He belonged to an Academic period when ordination was customary. Occasionally he took duty at some church: on one occasion he employed the spare moments of the function in rendering some of the *Te Deum* into

Classical Greek trochaic verse. This he finished later, and it is one of the most ingenious pieces in *Sabrinae Corolla*. On the whole old Shill was a pathetic figure. Into the notorious troubles of a mismanaged career I will not enter. You could not help liking him or feeling sorry for him. He would doubtless have been made Greek Professor in 1867, but the endowment of that office was mainly derived from a Canonry at Ely, and it was impossible to make Shilleto a Reverend Canon. The Fellows of Peterhouse saved Cambridge from the disgrace of ignoring a great scholar. They elected him to fill a vacant Fellowship. The event was sudden, but generally welcomed. One evening I went for my hour as usual, but he was not at home, a strange thing. Next morning I happened to be out, and met him near Trinity. He button-holed me with a grin and said 'Very sorry—elected Fellow of Peterhouse only yesterday—had to go and wet it.' Such was the man whose influence was dominant in the Classical school for many years, affecting not only students but examiners. The reaction against it was beginning, chiefly in Trinity, but elsewhere also.

In 1867 Trinity College had on its staff four notable old Salopians, Munro, W G Clark, E M Cope, Robert Burn. The editor of Lucretius needs no comment. W G Clark, who was Public Orator, had been an enterprising traveller in Greece, Poland, and Spain. Cope specialized on Plato and

Aristotle's Rhetoric, of which latter he left a classic edition. It was in reference to him that I was told a story. Two Fellow-Commoners coming out of his lecture room—A said to B 'does it awfully well, doesn't he?' B replied, lisping 'I suppose the poor miserable beggar gets his living by it.' Cope was sadly disappointed in not getting the Greek Professorship. Burn, author of *Rome and the Campagna*, was a fine figure of a Cambridge Don, a man much beloved. Beside these Salopians, there were other men of note—Henry Sidgwick, then becoming a leading philosopher; Jebb, unrivalled in the use of Greek; Henry Jackson, a hearty being, in touch with undergraduate life and thought, destined to many years of influence as an example of all that was straightforward and manly. The reputation of the Trinity team had a great effect outside in promoting movements of reform. But there were a few elsewhere working in the same direction, in particular at Christ's, where John Peile was hand in glove with the Trinity men. A very remarkable personage there was the Tutor and Classical lecturer W M Gunson, who had been dominant at Christ's for many years. Vastly self-confident, and proud of his native Cumberland, he was at no pains to dissemble the fact of his own honourable independence or to minimize his proper importance as a mainstay of the Cambridge Classical school. Perhaps no other man so perfectly illustrated the regular habits of a Don of the old type. Every day he took the same walk at the same pace, every evening his allowance of Port after Hall. Judged by the standards of his generation, he was a good scholar and a successful teacher. As examiner his methods were rather old-fashioned and mechanical, but in their own way sound. Of their infallibility he entertained (and expressed) no doubt whatever. Yet he was no obstructive, and was favourable to reform. Tall and spare in figure, he had something of a 'presence.' At times gruff and hard-spoken, he was really kind-hearted. He was in Holy Orders. A number of stories of his characteristic sayings and doings were current, but I abstain from repeating them.

AN EXAMINATION STORY

As I have referred to the justifiable pride of Cambridge men in their examination system, I think it may be not amiss to say something of a curious affair that caused much talk in 1882. The Examiners in the Classical Tripos of that year were convinced that one of the candidates had been guilty of foul play. Some parts of his work shewed that he had somehow got knowledge of passages to be set and had prepared them beforehand. Other parts betrayed a notable inability to deal with passages that to him were actually 'unseen,' and various alterations and errors of a suspicious character were detected. Being fully agreed that

the man (say X) ought not to have a Degree with
Honours on the strength of his performance, the
Examiners were in a dilemma. If they put his name
in the list, its place would be determined by the
marks assigned him; but they could not honestly
say that this represented their opinion of his merits.
Too scrupulous to put their signatures to a false
list, they at the same time shrank from omitting
the man's name on their own authority, as they
had power to do. So they turned to the Vice-
Chancellor for advice. The V C, a kindly well-
meaning man of more geniality than discretion,
authorized them to omit the name. This he had
no power to do, and with the publication of the
list troubles began. Mr X called on the Vice-
Chancellor, who answered his questions by in-
forming him that his name was omitted because
of his having employed unfair methods in the
examination. Both X and his father at once protested, and raised a storm. Then, having themselves
made the accusation public, they could hardly help
insisting that it was too serious to be left unproven.
Weeks of blustering outcry against injustice and
wrong done to a poor innocent student (a good
deal of it in print) followed. It was noticed that
direct denial of fraud was avoided, but so much
scandal was being created that the whole matter
had to be brought before the Council of the
Senate. Of this body I was the junior member.
Long debates made it clear that a mere refusal to

take any step would not meet the case. Things had gone too far. Eventually it was agreed to appoint a special court of referees, who should hear the available evidence and report to the University thereon. I was thirsting to get nominated on that body. I had fought against a mere *non possumus* dismissal of X's claims, but was morally certain that the Examiners had judged the man rightly. My own experience of teaching and examining, and acquaintance with the undergraduate mind, was recent and various, and I hoped to win the credit of exposing a rogue. But the true Academic spirit prevailed, and the choice fell upon men eminent enough and to spare, but above the possession of the qualifications just then needed.

The inquiry was held, and a very difficult business it must have been. The report did not acquit Mr X, but it admitted that his guilt could not be proved. A pitiful and insincere compromise followed. The man was admitted to a Degree by special Grace, but his name was not placed in the Tripos list. He presently disappeared from Cambridge, and rumour said that he came to a wretched end on the London Streets. But shortly after another person left Cambridge without much notice. This was a man in the employ of the University Press. How he came into the story there is no need to explain. I have some reason to believe that the most active of Graduates then resident had from the first his finger on the weak spot, but would not hastily expose the fraud, for fear of damaging the reputation of the Press. At all events the matter rested until the trouble was over, and the offender was removed, and the Press vindicated as an establishment trustworthy in the highest degree. The real go-between and organizer of this shameful affair was a disreputable Graduate, who also sought another sphere for his energies.

The whole episode was not without its lessons, of which the most agreeable was the vindication of Examiners' judgment as critics of the performance of candidates. In the circumstances, their attempt to share responsibility was a weakness that only men convinced of their own immunity from human error will refuse to condone. They had to deal with a shifty rogue, who stuck at nothing. One of his dodges was to make piteous appeals for advice to any person that he could find an excuse for addressing, and several Graduates suffered annoyance through his garbled versions of interviews. Hearing of this, I received him courteously, but at parting I insisted on giving him a written abstract of my advice, signed and dated, so that he could produce it if needed. He protested against causing me all this trouble, but he had to take the paper, and never ventured to quote me in any way. The injudicious innocence of the Examiners gave him some further opportunities of making points in his game, but I will not dwell on them. I had reason to know that undergraduate opinion pronounced him guilty from the first. And here ends an un-savoury story.

Such were some of the characters in the Classical school then just at the outset of a period of frequent changes. In one other department a movement was begun that interested me at the time. Modern History had been recognized as a fit subject of Academic study by the foundation of a Regius Professorship in 1724. But the appointment of Professors had been kept in the hands of the 'Crown,' the subject being one that might be so treated as to annoy the Government. Hence stagnation had long been normal. But recent Professors had at least begun to lecture, and official nervousness no longer required tameness as a qualification for the post. On Kingsley's death J R Seeley was in 1869 appointed to succeed him. From the new man much was expected, for he was known as a man of ideas, bent upon gaining for the study a strong and independent position. He gave an inaugural lecture in the Senate House to a large audience. I was present. While exerting himself to define the nature and range of the subject he did not shrink from assailing the narrowness of the Cambridge curriculum, in particular the Classical school, which he charged with excessive devotion to verbal scholarship and neglect of more important aspects of antiquity. And there was much truth in his accusation. The tradition of 'pure scholarship,' as carried on by Shilleto and many of

137

his pupils, did in fact need serious revision. But the utterances of the new evangelist were something of a shock to many old residents. It was on this occasion that Dr Thompson, Master of Trinity, in his usual sarcastic vein remarked 'I did not think we should have regretted Professor Kingsley so soon.' Nevertheless Seeley had not spoken in vain, and the following years saw great changes, both in the establishment of History as a study to be recognized by a Tripos and a Degree with Honours, and in an enlargement of the scope of the Classical Tripos. Truth is, opinion was ripe for a continuation of the onward movement started a few years earlier by the foundation of Triposes in Moral and Natural Sciences. Whether the separation of History from Law, and its subsequent combination with Archaeology, has been an unmixed benefit, is another question. That Seeley, a master of the art of lecturing, was too much devoted to a system of classification, premature and not always profound, is I think now generally admitted. But as a stimulating force in Academic life he did a service not to be forgotten.

Meanwhile a movement was in progress without which the reform of the Classical school would have been impossible. So long as teaching was almost entirely in the hands of the Colleges, and each College normally appointed as Lecturer the next apparently qualified man in their own body, it was inevitable that the official teachers should vary

greatly in earnestness and efficiency. I could illustrate this by a number of stories, but let it suffice
that some lecturers grossly neglected the due preparation of their subjects. Even in St John's I have
had to point out to a Lecturer that my exercise,
to which he had given unreserved praise, contained at least three prodigious blunders which I
had detected since it was written. Even that marvel
of learning John Mayor was not a success in the
lecture room. He only prepared his matter so far
as to set the tap running. The flow was impressive,
at times astounding. But it was all isolated detail,
with hardly any comment or criticism of his own.
So we got a mass beyond our digestion, and did
not get what we should have been eager to hear.
From what friends in other Colleges told me, it was
evident that St John's was comparatively well off
in respect of official teaching. The new movement
for intercollegiate lectures had its rise in Trinity,
supported by Christ's. A tentative step was the
admission to lectures of men from other Colleges
provided with cards of recommendation from their
several Tutors. As time went on, various formalities
were quietly dropped. So the present open system
came into being.

For my part I can only say that I lost no time in
getting a share of the proffered boon, and was not
disappointed. Of the three lecturers to whom I
listened in Trinity, Jackson Jebb and Sidgwick,
all good, the last was in my opinion far the best.

I came away convinced that there were in a lecture-room possibilities of which much might be made, and that the able and learned Johnian staff were somehow hampered by their system or by the spirit in which it was worked. The latter alternative was the true one. It was in fact the custom, not peculiar to St John's, to regard an office as a sort of freehold, and in appointments to consider first who had the strongest claim to a vacant post, not what sort of man was needed to fill it. No doubt the rule of seniority applicable to College Livings carried great weight in a predominantly clerical society. Most Fellows were waiting their turn for the offer of a benefice, and looked upon a College office as similarly due to them in their turn, a post in which they might make some savings, ready for the time when an opening for preferment (and marriage) should occur. Whether this or that Lecturer were in such a position of expectancy or not, mattered little. It was the atmosphere created by circumstances that had a deadening effect. I recall a striking case. The College Educational Board recommended a certain person for appointment to a lectureship. The Governing Body a few hours later ignored this, and promptly used their power to appoint instead a man, of great merit it is true, but who was not judged the most suitable by the educational staff, and who did not himself seek appointment. As to 'atmosphere,' take this case in illustration. A Fellow who had not resided since his election, having been on Church duty elsewhere, came back to reside in College, meaning to take a Living when a chance should occur. His inexperience in College details may be gathered from the fact that when the Butler announced in Hall 'there will be a Sealing in the Combination Room after Hall,' he remarked 'I thought there was one there already.' In perfect good faith he thought of a ceiling, knowing nothing of the formal act of affixing the College Seal to documents. Now to this worthy man it seemed certain that, having taken first-class Honours, and being now high on the roll of Fellows by lapse of time, he would have the first offer of a vacant Lectureship. So he took a large set of rooms, and actually fitted up one room for a lecture class in the style then usual. True, his assumption was never put to the test, for a timely vacancy soon transferred him to a parochial charge. I well remember the amusement caused by the whole episode.

THE COMING OF REFORM

These stories sound like fiction, but they are only the bare truth. I may be told that they do not redound to the credit of St John's, and ought to have been left to wholesome oblivion. I do not think so. St John's was the first College to improve its teaching and examining, in the latter part of the eighteenth century, a practical protest against the torpor of the age. It could not keep the first place for ever, but it did keep it for many years, and is very strong now. Trinity woke up and turned to account its exceptional advantages. The stagnation that tended to impair the vigour of St John's was comparatively recent, largely due to certain changes in the Governing Body, which in my early College days was controlled by a narrow-minded and bigoted clique. They passed on to it by seniority and were unremovable: and the mischief they did lived after they had ceased to rule. That things were somehow kept going, and the College held its own high position, was first and foremost due to the Master Dr Bateson, whose skill in managing an untoward crew of Seniors was wonderful. But he could not always lead them straight, and the fruits of their misrule gave trouble after his death.

The Statutes of 1860 had introduced many changes into the various Colleges. Some effects of these were beginning to appear; but in general it must be admitted that the movement worked tardily. Vested interests were not extinguished, and reformers had an uphill game. I recall the cases of three Colleges whose doings were of more than ordinary importance, as it seemed to me. King's, led by the Tutor, Augustus Austen Leigh, was thrown open to students other than those from Eton. This momentous development was already at work, destined to produce the present society, intellectual above all things, and notable for keeping the pursuit of athletic distinction duly subordinate to its main objects. Trinity Hall had for some years been under the guidance of its great Tutor H Latham. He was a remarkable figure, unrivalled in the power of controlling full-blooded Undergraduates. No man understood better the need of enforcing order and obedience; no man saw more clearly that petty regulations and frequent interference only serve to make dignity ridiculous and corrupt the moral bonds of discipline. The Hall had no large funds available for the relief of poor students, and I believe I am doing 'Ben' (as he was called) no wrong in saying that he thought enough was done on those lines in some other Colleges—perhaps too much, for endowment of mediocre ability was a policy that could easily be carried too far. On the other hand, to bring young men together and keep them out of mischief (a vastly important matter), was a function not always performed by College Tutors with success. So he made it his business to encourage all forms of bodily exercise, above all rowing. He abhorred slackness of any kind, and his contempt for humbug led shallow observers to regard him as a cynic. That he took thought for the Poll men did not imply indifference to intellectual pursuits. In his hands the Hall produced several men of high distinction both in Academic Honours and in Literature and public life. No man was less of a snob, but he never

viewed high station or wealth as social defects: he
was bound to do his best for the rich as much as
for the poor. It was only in his later years that
outsiders fairly appreciated his intense dislike of
cant, which dislike was nothing but an outward
expression of profound religion. He was known to
have made a fortune by shrewd investments. But
not less shrewd was the discriminating benevolence
expressed in his Will. The third College to which I
refer was Jesus, where an old Salopian, H A Morgan,
was making a fine effort as Tutor to reform and
develope his College on much the same lines as
Trinity Hall. A succession of rowing victories put
Jesus at the head of the river and led to a period
of signal prosperity. But a reaction followed a too
speedy advance. I think the fall was mainly due
to the ill-judged haste-to-glory policy of a col-
league, not to H A M himself. Anyhow the tide
has long ago ceased to ebb.

TESTS AND CELIBACY

I have dwelt upon these cases because I took at
the time a deep interest in them all. Of course
I could not appreciate the full significance of the
movement of which they were early symptoms.
Though the chief movers were clergy, that was
merely the result of old Statutes. Laymen were
already beginning to find a place on College staffs.
The old excess of resident Fellows in Orders, either

waiting for ecclesiastical preferment or consuming years in sterile nullity, had been condemned by public opinion. But the religious Test still remained, and in most Colleges the rule of celibacy. Public opinion was ripe for another move onward. In 1871 the Test was abolished, a great relief to me personally, as it enabled me to hold a Fellowship. How stubbornly the old exclusive spirit still lurked in certain circles, may be judged from what happened to me. Hitherto all Fellows of Colleges had on admission not only to make a Test-declaration to their several Masters, but also to sign a form in a book kept by the Vice-Chancellor. From these bonds I was free, and in College the Master simply struck out the Test clauses of the statutory declaration and admitted me under the unrepealed remainder. But all men were not so straightforward as Dr Bateson. A private message was brought me from the V C (that is, from the clique who were pressing him,) that, if I wished to sign in the customary way, he would be very happy to receive me. Of course I declined the offer, but I believe there were some who accepted it. In a few years this absurd attempt was dropped. The opposition to Tests had been for some time gaining strength within the University, Trinity as usual being the headquarters of the movement under the leadership of some notable men: the relief, sadly overdue, was hastened by the quiet self-sacrifice of Henry Sidgwick, the author of a pamphlet on the Ethics of Conformity and

Subscription, who resigned his Fellowship on the ground that he could no longer remain pledged by the Test. This species of Academic martyrdom had a striking effect. For many a long day it had not unnaturally been usual to regard College endowments as a permanent provision for those who won a share in them. Either a man (unmarried of course) remained a Fellow for life, or he went off to a College Living or some other preferment. Tenure for a limited term of years, introduced by Statutes of 1860, was a new notion. Many men were sick of the Test-system, but something of a shock was needed to arouse keen interest in the matter. Sidgwick did what was lacking, and the cause triumphed.

There was still the question of celibacy, and the removal of this monastic restriction was also long overdue. Opposition however was strong. A favourite argument was that, if men could marry and yet hold Fellowships, the vacancies would be much fewer. Now to many it seemed that nothing kept intellectual emulation alive so effectively as the hope of succession to a Fellowship. Some also urged that from the public point of view these prizes were doing as great a national service in the hands of non-residents as in those of residents. They enabled young men to tide over the first unproductive years of a professional career, especially at the Bar. The usefulness of residents was in comparison minimized; and indeed there were cases that might justify the sneer. At the back of it all was the undisguised prize-system by which Fellowships were made rewards of 'merit'; that is, of high places in Triposes. Use had created a habit of mind. If a man won a place such as his College generally requited with a Fellowship, he was felt to have a claim to it, and was free after election to do what he would with his own, so long as he broke no Statute. This habit had been outgrown by Trinity, where the Society determined elections by tests of their own and not by Tripos places. It was not until the Statutes of 1882 that marriage was generally permitted. From that time the old prize-system steadily died down under the growth of new ideas. Cambridge took off its coat, and set to work in earnest to meet the requirements of the age. Without the pressure of public opinion, embodied in legislative acts, nothing like the present results could have been attained.

At this point I cannot help making some remarks on the effects, direct and indirect, of the abolition of statutory celibacy. The restriction had long been resented by individuals, and H A Morgan had even written a pamphlet on the subject. But the growth of a body of opinion favourable to abolition was slower than might have been expected. The large class of residents connected with the work of Laboratories and Museums, now so great a voting power, did not exist in the sixties of last century. There were a few officials, and what was being done was partly done by unpaid workers. Salaries of paid workers were low, not suggestive of matrimony. Money was tied up in the Colleges, and Colleges were in general apathetic. In most of these Societies the majority were either men in Orders or lay bachelors inured to the denial of home life and content to find in College privileges and perquisites a sufficient compensation. The total number of resident Graduates was something over 200. The drowsy simplicity of Academic life shewed itself in the persistence of the traditional Vice-Chancellor's dinners. In theory (I cannot answer for the practice) the V C invited all residents once in each year. Invitations were sent round by the Marshal, by whose favour you could learn who were to be of the company on a given day. If in his good graces, you might even arrange a transfer, as I once discovered for my own convenience. Beside residents, there would now and then be others in town on their several occasions—*commorantes in villa* was the official description—and these so-called 'cormorants' were often included in the parties. Some men declined these invitations; why, I know not, unless it were from pity for the host. The custom is now long obsolete.

The position of the average clerical Fellow was much like this. There was a demand for more Science, and generally for more specialized activity. To grant this, and allow marriage, meant that men would pass their lives in Academic work, in fact would become professionals. Now for those who had been used to succeed automatically to College posts tenable during their years of waiting, or to see their neighbours doing the same, this prospect had little attraction. No man cares to see his own scheme of life treated by implication as useless or out of date. Moreover, the demanded reform was according to old prepossessions an attack upon the Church. Ever since 1688 the Establishment, however spiritually tepid it might at any moment be, had clung to its endowments and its privileges without serious challenge. And its hold on the Universities was a right of no small value. Already the Statutes of 1860 had given laymen a foothold: was it desirable that they should be put in full possession of the Colleges? Sentiments of this kind, not always openly expressed, undoubtedly had much weight. But things had gone too far for effective opposition. The Irish Church and Land Acts of 1868–70 were a warning; those for the abolition of Purchase in the Army and of University Tests followed in 1871. Cambridge was to be utilized by being brought into closer touch with national life. Resident Graduates were to serve their country in the duties that they were best fitted to perform. To impose celibacy on its citizens was impossible for a state that required their services. So it was abolished in 1882 to the common benefit of Church and State.

It would give a wrong impression to lay the blame of opposition to reform on the clerical Dons as such. Some of the most cynical opponents were laymen of hearty secularity. These were few in number, but solidly proof against argument, public opinion, and things of that kind. To a man with an assured position and free scope for indulging his fancies, inclined to what is called 'Sport,' the nearness of Cambridge to Newmarket and London was a great convenience. Some had borne an active part in their earlier days; but addiction to such pursuits is seldom a blessing when continued passively in middle age. Some, with no sporting record of their own, had a fancy for judging and backing their own judgment. Of whatever special type, the sporting man likes a good dinner and has now and again some 'event' to celebrate. Habits are formed not suited to Academic life nowadays. Even then these men were out of date, stray survivals of the old social conditions depicted by Gunning. Some were good fellows at bottom, some not. The worst of the set was not a layman. He was said to have been a hard-working curate, and to have been spoilt by his election to a Fellowship. Formerly athletic, he was in my time known chiefly as an authority on eating and drinking. Another was famed for the same accomplishments, combined with a portentous memory for past scandals, and his conversation was amusing, if not always edifying. Another was associated with billiard-rooms and Newmarket, and noted for the remarkable accuracy of his forecasts and estimates, such

as judging weights, predicting results, and the like·
One rather younger than the rest was a genuine
Sportsman, a hard rider to hounds, apt to be
excessive in his relaxations after hunting, broad in
language and unrivalled in quick repartee. In his
character native honesty unchecked had bred a
deep contempt for humbug, which he detected in
the solemn society around him, sometimes too
hastily. A scornful attitude expressed itself unhappily in self-depreciation. Those who knew him
were aware that his representation of himself did
not give you the real man. Refusing to pose as being
what he was not, he concealed real generosity under
a mask of selfishness and dissembled his deep sense
of honour. But for him as for the other Bohemians
the times were not propitious, and his end was sad.
When the news came that Jack Perkins had shot
himself, pious Graduates shrugged their shoulders,
but some of us, Publicans and Sinners, received it
with sorrow.

I might run on to almost any length if I jotted
down my recollections of men important in their
influence on Academic life but not striking figures
in connexion with this or that notable achievement.
But I have to be content with a few words. Few
of the older survivors will forget Henry Fawcett
of Trinity Hall for many years Professor of Political
Economy. He was most widely known as a Liberal
M P, and eventually as Postmaster General. His
loss of sight through an accident, and his brave

struggle to overcome the calamity, made him an object of deep sympathy and respect. He stuck at nothing. In the crew of 'Ancient Mariners' that used to be seen on the river, their blind Stroke was a general favourite. He rode and skated with perfect fearlessness, though one learnt that his companions found him rather a dangerous partner on horseback or on the ice. He managed to get over the difficulties of dining in Hall, and was everywhere a cheery presence. His Liberalism was sorely strained in Academic politics, for he did not welcome changes in Cambridge. But to the last he was a popular figure, and his funeral at Trumpington was a great demonstration of public sorrow. There was also at Trinity Hall a meagre and reticent man, known to few outside but a notable character, F L Hopkins. I regret that I never drew him out to tell the story of his travels. In the days of Ottoman rule he had made long journeys in the Balkan countries. It was known that he had been nursed through a serious illness by the daughter of a Bulgarian farmer, whose devoted care he wished to requite. Money, it was said, was not an appropriate reward, but the lady asked for a memento that took her fancy—the tall hat which Hopkins wore in every company and clime, as he did in Cambridge. He wrote a little Turkish grammar.

At the same College was Edward Carpenter, for some years in Holy Orders and doing duty at St Edward's Church. Later on he gave up the ecclesiastical position and withdrew to become a priest of social improvement on hand-labour lines. I believe he still cultivates a piece of land round his cottage in Yorkshire, earning his living by his own hands, a missionary by example. His is a case illustrating the searchings of heart that came upon many men in the seventies of last century.

At King's there was Henry Bradshaw the University Librarian, a typical man of learning, devoted to duty and ever ready to put his store at the service of others. Of this universally beloved character I need say no more. The fine frame and genial presence of the Bursar Frederick Whitting are not lightly to be forgotten. He was one of the few who seemed never more at ease than on horseback. As a typical English Gentleman he was (as such men always will be) a valuable member of Academic society. Oscar Browning came back into residence after his disagreement with the Head of Eton, and entered on a long period of agitation in Cambridge. He has left us his own story told from his own point of view. My view of him is that, in spite of many weaknesses and occasional follies, he did on the whole good service in stirring up the Cambridge pool, always in danger of stagnation. Of the admirable Augustus Austen Leigh I have spoken above.

Memory is apt to recall figures of those who bore a part in forwarding or hindering the general Academic movements of their time. But I must not forget that there were men not less notable, indeed perhaps more so, who played their parts without becoming involved in the controversial activities of an age of reform. Of one of these, E H Palmer the Lord Almoner's Reader or Professor of Arabic and Fellow of St John's, I must say a few words. His career and his tragic end in the service of his country [1882] have been described in his *Life* by Sir Walter Besant, a truly wonderful story. What concerns me here is my recollection of him as a singularly unacademic character in an Academic setting. His was a case in which the College system shewed what it could do at its best. To St John's he owed the solid encouragement that enabled him to develope his extraordinary linguistic gifts, and he passed a number of years in College rooms. His delicate health unfitted him for the exacting routine of some jostling profession. As a College Fellow he was free to ignore uncongenial and un-profitable clashings of Academic opinion and follow his own bent. There was one emotion—Surprise—which nothing ever seemed able to arouse in him: the commonplace limits of the possible and probable were ignored with unruffled calm. He could give quite different versions of a thing to different men, not from indifference to truth, but rather from an Eastern sense of propriety; thus Messrs A B C etc each got what suited his particular case, in short what he deserved. Each would receive the same gentle smile, backed by the raising of the eyebrows that Palmer's friends knew so well. No pretence or humbug could escape him; and when he took to water-colour drawing he could not resist the temptation to caricature. College Meetings he loathed. Once he was induced to attend one on Statute-reform. After a short time he rose and left with apology to the Master for a pressing engagement. It turned out afterwards that he had just caught the outline of an honoured senior Fellow, and had hurried away to get the sketch done while the impression was fresh.

I must not suggest that in his hands caricature was ill-natured. Even when there were two versions of a portrait, the one not meant for the victim's eye was no more than a subtle record of little peculiarities cleverly caught. A reasonable man happening to see this portrait of himself might well take it with a good-humoured laugh. The calm elusive nature of Palmer was displayed in his conjuring skill. In a crowded room with men touching his elbows he would perform trick after trick, completely baffling the curiosity of the company, doing things that noted professionals would only attempt behind a special table and at some little distance. Needless to say that he had no belief in the genuineness of the phenomena paraded by the Spiritualists. Some of their most surprising effects were reproduced by him as results of simple conjuring. Perhaps these reminiscences of an extraordinary man are not irrelevant to my attempt at depicting Cambridge as I saw it years ago. That the greatest linguist in the University, and the man with the deftest fingers, was looking on at all our doings with a calm smile of indifference, is a fact that I cannot forget.

I have tried to sketch truthfully the state of opinion and the tone of resident society in the years when the revolution of 1882 was preparing. There were of course many men holding a middle position, and others who accepted the necessity of reform but were concerned to support it only if 'moderate.' Such is, and I suppose always will be, the attitude of those who are fairly satisfied with the state of things in which they have themselves thriven. But I do not remember any serious utterance of a 'cry' that has been more than once heard in later years,—I mean 'Let us settle these matters among ourselves'; that is, by voting in the Senate. If my memory be not utterly at fault, there was a general conviction, tacit or expressed, that external pressure, however unwelcome, was unavoidable. Opposition to inquiry by Commission was slight and of course futile. The letters of Dr Phelps, Master of Sidney, in answer to questions, were the most striking assertions of die-hard obstruction, and it was remarked at the time that what they said was not more significant than what they did not say. In some Colleges the inquiry was positively welcomed, and it was generally known that Trinity was disarming compulsion by preparing measures for setting its own house in order. In St John's things did not begin to move until the Act of 1877 was passed. Then we went through two or three years of conflict. The opposition was strong, not only in numbers. Some non-resident Fellows, young barristers, fought hard for the interests of their class, and their training gave them a great advantage in dealing with men of purely Academic experience. However, in the end we bowed to the inevitable in most respects. Some unwise clauses in our Statutes were allowed by the Commission to stand, but have either been amended later or have proved unworkable.

To give any adequate picture of the activities that followed the revolution of 1882 is far beyond my power. Cambridge was a scene of projects and claims jostling each other in eager competition. The machinery of University government was sorely strained, and became more and more complex as needs became more pressing. 'University business' was no longer a lesiurely process carried on by a few easy-going magnates, but a monstrous burden, as it is now. The Reformers, mostly men already busy, bore their part manfully and unpaid. The discontented looked on and sneeringly criticized the policy that was involving the University in debt. For without borrowing large sums no progress was possible. I smile when I recall such utterances as 'here we are mortgaging the Library and the Senate House to raise money for buildings in which men are to do what they could do elsewhere just as well, or better.' But that was the sort of comment that one heard, only varying in detail; and old-fashioned mathematicians were every bit as cynical as the benighted members of the literary schools. To such grumbling and to much indifference the Reformers paid little heed. They went ahead, and the new Financial Board shewed itself well able to grapple with the problems before it. From that time to this the work has gone on steadily. Naturally most of the new undertakings were connected with scientific departments, developing those in being and establishing new. To me the whole movement was not so much of a surprise as it seemed to be to some of my friends. I had made one or two trips to Germany, and in 1876 at Leipsic I got a copy of the official announcement of the year's routine. It opened my eyes to several things, particularly to the vast number and variety of the courses offered in Natural Sciences, as compared with the literary schools, though these too were far more liberally staffed than the corresponding departments at Cambridge. And I knew enough of Germany to feel sure that all this elaborate provision was not a pretentious sham. The lesson made me a steady backer of onward movements at home, and in what I had already seen of Cambridge life there was nothing to make me view regretfully the old conditions that were passing away. And now in 1924, when the scientific equipment is drawing near completion, I cannot see that the fear of other subjects being swamped by the flood of the Sciences is justified. Much more in evidence is the innocent precocity that nowadays leads all studies to don the robe and name of Science. If this be their ultimate Academic Dress, what harm if in some cases it begins by being a disguise?

THE PROGRESS OF REFORM

The years of remodelling that followed 1882 were a most interesting period. The events as they occurred were duly recorded in the *Reporter*. That organ was itself founded in 1870 to meet a want that was beginning to be felt. It had been the custom to send round notices of University matters on printed slips to the several Colleges, an inadequate method, which was found to be occasionally inconvenient. An attempt to supply a better means of circulation was made in the shape of an University Gazette. As a private enterprise this quickly failed, and the *Reporter* 'published by Authority' took its place. A quaint specimen of Academic precision was the view of Dr Luard the Registrary that, though published by Authority, it was not Official. I have always taken this to mean that it can conceivably err, while 'Official' implies or at least suggests Infallible. Whether this distinction is still cherished in high quarters, I cannot say. The occasional issue of amended Tripos lists is an illustration of the point. The generation now

in harness has been reared on the *Reporter*, and the
rise in number of resident Graduates from something over 200 to over 800 makes it a necessity of
Academic life. We have recently witnessed the
transformation of another relic of the old simple
ways in the case of the *Calendar*. It was nothing but
a private venture on which great pains were spent.
The publishers got their details from the University
and College officials, and the work was noted for
its accuracy. But it grew in size so fast that the
price had to be raised, and it ceased to pay. Since
then (1913) it has given place to official publica-
tions in more than one volume.

So things moved on, and Progressives such as
Coutts Trotter and James Stuart were wondrous
busy with the new developments. But it would give
a false impression to imply that the men of advanced views had a free hand so far as to carry out
their plans unchecked. Direct opposition was futile,
but Progressive policy was liable to error through
haste and enthusiasm. By watching opportunities
it was possible now and then to modify its action
in a conservative sense. This could only be done
by bearing a part in Academic business of every
kind, by giving well-timed proofs of exceptional
capacity, and turning chances to account. Not all
the reformers had the patience to study details outside the sphere of their own special departments,
or the imagination to forecast the probable effect
of one change on the prospects of another. Few

indeed had the physical vigour to remain alert and clear-sighted, ready with a policy, when dealing with complicated affairs in wearisome meetings. The man who met these requirements came not from Trinity but from St Catharine's. G F Browne, known to all the University as the prince of Proctors, and as manager of the Local Examinations to a large part of the British world, was certainly in the period of which I am speaking the most important single figure in Cambridge life. No other man so fully grasped the truth that the value and bearing of institutions depends on the agents who work them; or the corollary that the competence necessary to success is increased by varied and thorough experiences. He had served the Commissioners of 1877–82 as Secretary. Year after year he was an active member of the Council of the Senate and endless Syndicates and Committees, everywhere contributing to the achievement of maximum results with minimum waste of time. Hence he gained an influence never paraded but almost always effectual. He accepted responsibility without a gesture of self-sacrifice, and in his hands responsibility carried with it the power of exercising a judicious control. An instance of this occurred when James Stuart set going the movement for Local Lectures. Browne cleared away initial difficulties by getting the scheme linked with the Local Examinations in one office, where he had an organized staff that only needed a slight increase for the time being. Thus the Progressives were obliged by facilitation of the start, while the employment of suitable lecturers was in practice mainly controlled by a Conservative hand. I need not enlarge on this or other illustrations of his far-reaching activities. Well do I remember a conversation I heard between two residents. A. 'I met a foreigner in the street, who asked me to shew him the University. I didn't know what to do: what would you have done?' B. 'I should have introduced him to G F Browne.'

Now, why am I dwelling so long on the position of one individual? Because in his interesting Reminiscences Bishop Browne does justice to his own manifold occupations while in residence here, but does not lay enough stress on what seems to me the most interesting point about them. He was a strong and determined Churchman, in a society still abounding in Clerics, mostly weak, some luke-warm, all painfully conscious that they were no longer in the seat of power. The presence of so surefooted a leader was to them an encouragement in a time of trial. It helped to abate dissension, to reconcile the clergy to the inevitable, and so to smooth the transition to the new state of things. No doubt the great Divines of the period saw the value of his services, and their support gave him additional strength. A firm disciplinarian to all who had to work under him, he was the very leader then required to redeem the Conservative forces, clerical or lay, from undue disheartenment, and deserved praise from any candid observer. I had many opportunities of studying his methods. To watch him manipulating a committee of any kind was an instructive experience. The guidance of discussion, the skilful choice of the right moment to invite the opinion of a particular person, or to offer a solution of some difficulty, were truly admirable as patterns of a rare but useful art. On the Local Examinations Syndicate these gifts were most conspicuous. The usual result was that he, the Secretary, loyally carried out in his office decisions of a body that had been led to adopt them through his judicious management. Naturally there were a few occasions when Progressive members grew restive at something that thwarted their wishes, but they seldom had the equipment to enable them to escape the control of their real master. As to office discipline there was no sort of doubt. For instance, the Presiding Examiners at Local Centres were held on a tight rein. I speak from experience. A significant detail was the selection of men to be sent to particular centres. I remember that on two occasions my discharge of this duty led to the exposure of great slackness on the part of one Local Secretary and the vindication of another. When a cynical friend afterwards pointed out to me that I had been chosen as one likely to bring matters to a crisis, in short as a tool of the office, I was for the moment nettled:

but I soon assuaged my injured vanity by taking it as a compliment. Of strange experiences at Local Centres I have first and last had my full share: the worst of all is too unsavoury for repetition.

There were however some episodes that had a comic side, and in the general development of educational organization throughout the country are perhaps not likely to occur again. It used to be one of the regulations that 'Juniors' had to read aloud in the presence of the examiner. This was in the case of the girls sometimes a trying ordeal. Some were nervous in face of a stranger, and did not do themselves justice. It was hardly human to reject them on the ground of inability to read, if timidity were the real difficulty: and gentle encouragement was not always successful. With the bold there was no trouble. Most embarrassing was a little maid whose appealing innocence shewed that she would prefer to sit on my knee during the performance. I do not wonder that the reading regulation has been abolished. A troublesome case arose at a large centre (boys) in Lancashire. The Local Secretary, a parson, had engaged a large public room for the examination. Several irregularities had to be corrected at the cost of much friction. But, this done, a worse remained. The Hall had only been let for the purpose with reservation of one evening, when it was already bespoken for a concert. Of this I was not told till noon on that very day, when I was informed that the evening paper would be set in a parish schoolroom a little distance away. I protested against the suddenness of the change, but went to the place named at the appointed hour. There I found the boys crowded together so tight that they could hardly use their pens. There was no pretence of observing the most vital regulations. I pointed out that this would vitiate the whole examination. The Reverend Secretary replied that he could do no better. Duty at a funeral had hindered him, and he begged me to let the error pass. Now it was not on him, but on the boys, that the consequences of my refusal would fall: moreover, I was not sent there to act the prig, but to see things through if possible. So I found a way out of the mess to my own grave discomfort. I insisted on a music-stool being brought and set on a table in the middle of the room. On this I sat, ready to faint from the foulness of the air and the heat of the flaring gas lamps, and quietly revolved, watching the writers. Only thus could I certify my belief that there had been no corrupt practices. Indeed at some centres you earned your fee hardly.

One occasional function of resident life was (and is) the discussion of Reports presented to the Senate. These meetings are necessary, but sometimes wearing. One pities Vice-Chancellors who have to sit on while members try each other's patience. Yet I have known a Vice-Chancellor contribute to the confusion of a debate on a matter of practical policy. He intervened to state his own view, thus weakening his own moral power of control as chairman, and this not as a final word, but in the middle of the discussion. Not long before, he had put out a flysheet containing an opinion exactly opposite to that he now expressed. A copy of this document was in the room, in possession of a member present. This a member read out to him (of course without mention of the signature) and asked what he thought of it. The scene was not edifying, but it did save further waste of time. On another occasion the necessity of discussion was illustrated by sheer accident. A proposal from an important Syndicate contemplated a serious change in the conditions of employment in a certain great department, affecting the holidays of a whole staff of subordinates. Nobody seemed to object to the scheme. Happening to be present on other business, I rose and said 'I presume that the persons affected have been consulted as to the proposed change.' An indirect reply from a member of the Syndicate convinced me that I had not drawn my bow at a venture for nothing. So I pressed my question more pointedly. The eminent but choleric gentleman became angry, but had to admit that the staff concerned had had no opportunity of expressing their views. The meeting shewed signs of uneasiness at this disclosure. Little more was said, but the proposal, a most inequitable

one, was quietly dropped. In general I would remark that the absence of any power to introduce
amendments often limits the utility of these dis-
cussions. But how to confer such a power without
its accompanying drawbacks is a problem to be left
for solution by the wise.

Just a word on the Library. The rights of taking
out books and of personal access to the shelves are
simply priceless. So far as I know, our privileges
are unexampled elsewhere. But certain persons
have a nasty and dishonest habit of defacing the
text of books not their own by marks and notes
scribbled therein. I have taken careful notice of
cases that have come before me for many years.
It seems to me certain that young students are
not the guilty parties. Most of the notes are cor-
rections of supposed errors, but some of these only
intensify errors or introduce new ones. They are
the work of self-satisfied Graduates unrestrained
by doubts of their own infallibility. Now and then
I have strong reason to suspect that a book has
been used by a teacher of pupils, and marked and
noted in such a way as to facilitate its use for that
purpose. But most of this scribbling is the mere
output of conceit, in fact only pardonable when a
man is owner of the book he defaces. To detect
culprits is almost impossible: but, if the excellent
Library Staff ever do lay their hands on such an
offender, I trust means will be found of inflicting
exemplary punishment.

All the improvements made in the period of which I speak called for money. And this money, there being then no grant from Government, had to be got out of the Colleges. Now in Statutes there was generally some provision contemplating a future rise of income; seldom, if ever, any preparation to meet the contingency of a fall. Yet a grave depression of trade was already in full swing in 1879, and an even more alarming depression in agriculture followed. It was the normal practice of College finance (not an original design, but legalized by modern Statutes) to distribute the yearly balance among Fellows as a Dividend. The Statutes of 1882, starting from this basis, made the payment of the College contribution to the University a charge ranking as prior to Dividend. The result was that the dividends of the Fellows bore the whole brunt of the great Depression. In some Colleges the blow was severely felt, for instance in King's, Queens', and St John's. I may mention that the Johnian dividend, which in my earlier years had been £300, went on falling till somewhere in the nineties it was £80 for two consecutive years. It must be remembered that salaries of officers were based on the assumption that a Fellow's Dividend would be a leading item in their remuneration. To raise salaries now would, in the circumstances, lower the Dividend of all Fellows. The outlook was indeed black, and the fact of some Colleges being hard hit while some others were immune did not tend to contentment in general or comfort the sufferers. So serious was the situation that an attempt was made by H Sidgwick and a few comrades to arrange a voluntary composition by which the prosperous Colleges should bear a larger share of the common burdens than the Statutes required. It was however not possible to procure any general consent to accept charitable aid, and the generous design came to nothing.

In view of the changed position in recent years, owing to the Government grants made since the war, it may be well to repeat that all the developments of this reform-period were effected solely by the use of existing resources. Capital was raised by pledging the College contributions and whatever other means the University had at disposal as security for loans. This was a practical recognition of the now accepted principle that the University was no longer to be crippled by poverty while the Colleges looked on in endowed comfort. It was evident that for development of common efficiency it was vain to rely on the support of private benefactors. Long tradition had attached men to their several Colleges rather than to the University as a whole. Nor were they in general convinced that the conditions prevalent in their own day could be changed for the better. This attitude has not greatly changed in the last forty years. Gifts and bequests still go chiefly to Colleges, often to those Colleges that need them least: and the benefactor is apt to tie up his benefaction so strictly as to prevent a College from making the best use of the endowment. That he should wish to make it a memorial of himself is perhaps natural, but the conditions of bequests are sometimes quite grotesque in their minute detail. Some day men may learn that the best and most patriotic course is to leave coming generations a free hand in the use of endowments. But that day is not yet; and in order to work Cambridge up to its full capacity it is necessary to rely on money raised by public taxation.

There are some to whom this necessity seems deplorable, and who forebode evils arising from future Government interference as an inevitable corollary of Government support. But they do not, and I fear cannot, produce a practical alternative, and the reason is not far to seek. Underlying this question is the fact of which we are dimly conscious, but of which we do not often boast, that we Academics do not readily move on to meet the requirements of our own time. We have to be pushed from outside: the internal reformers are normally a minority. Our own Non-residents, including nearly all our wealthy men, are not as a rule desirous of change, and differ among themselves as to the direction that change should take, if change there is to be. When outside pressure forces us to move, these men generally prefer to look on. Loyalty to their old University does not necessarily express itself in enthusiasm for change;

if it reaches the stage of self-sacrifice in that cause, it will be too late, and the work has been already done without their aid.

Speaking as a Resident recalling memories of nearly sixty years, I sometimes wonder whether we Residents understand ourselves. There have always been men sincerely devoted to their duty in their several departments, and free from the bigotry that denies the possibility of any general change for the better. One of the best men I have ever known said to me in the seventies of last century 'I wish reformers would let us alone for a bit, and leave us free to do some work.' This was the utterance of one whose conscience was clear. But to comply with the wish of such a man meant in effect something further, unhappily inconsistent with his virtuous claim. It meant that men of a more bigoted type, prepossessed with obsolete ideas and indifferent to the needs of the present, would be kept in continual control of University policy. It was clear that the attitude of my friend was serving to reinforce a dead conservatism of which he and his like were no fit representatives. The same phenomenon may be observed in the Academic world of today with very slight difference of detail. The earnest worker is apt to be so engrossed in the promotion of his own work that he does not quite make allowance for the claims of other interests. Therefore any little movement of reaction gains strength from the support of men who have no real sympathy with it. A good instance of this may be found in a little matter of internal policy. A few years ago it was proposed to open the Fitzwilliam Museum on Sunday afternoons, and the Syndicate in charge had made careful arrangements to insure that the attendant staff should not suffer by the proposed change. Considering what had already been done in this direction elsewhere, the contemplated step was on the face of it innocent enough. And yet it was fanatically opposed on grounds that were at least mainly if not wholly sabbatarian in spirit. I record this in shame, for I did not vote, and regret my abstention. Honour to those who did take part in a hard-won victory, and gave Cambridge what is a real if modest boon.

In looking back on the changes effected under the new Statutes it seems to me that the work done was in variety and volume much greater than the younger generation can imagine or appreciate. To the labours of his predecessors the gifted Graduate pays small regard, and accepts the fruits of past energy and self-sacrifice as a mere matter of course. I have even heard sneering references to the reformers who toiled faithfully for the benefit of an age they could not hope to see, and without pay or reward of any kind. That in accomplishing so much they should now and then make mistakes was humanly inevitable. It was not wonderful that in the erection of so many new buildings unfortunate accidents should occur. One affair in particular[1] well illustrates the disadvantage at which all corporate bodies stand in dealing with individuals. A building was needed to house a scientific department, and it was important to make it secure against the risk of fire. It was accordingly designed with fire-proof floors and roof, constructed of concrete in which iron girders were to be imbedded. Shortly after these were laid, while a party of workmen were on the roof, a mass of this suddenly gave way, and passed downwards, carrying with it corresponding parts of the floors, until it reached the bottom. I believe no one was seriously hurt. But of course the whole policy of the structure was called in question. The accident had occurred in February 1878, and months passed in consulting eminent experts, who at first were content with recommending half-measures. They found neither the concrete nor the girders quite satisfactory, but thought that with some strengthenings and additions the work might be carried to a successful end. As time went by, and further disquieting signs appeared, they took a stronger tone. The architect held that his design was blameless: the concrete and the girders were together adequate, each strengthening the other. Evidently this put the blame on the contractors, as having supplied defective material. But the experts replied that neither element of the structure was by itself really

[1] Details in the *Cambridge University Reporter* 1878–81.

adequate: therefore neither had strength to spare for supporting the other. An engineering specialist was of opinion that false economy had been the prime cause of the trouble, but he too at first recommended adherence to the original design, with better materials and extra precautions.

Meanwhile the Syndicate in charge (a strong body) were becoming uneasy. While agreeing to follow the engineer's advice, they put on record their opinion that the University was not liable for the additional expense that the disaster and its remedies would surely cause. This left the blame to be shared between architect and contractors. But the remains of the faulty structure did not cease to develope defects. In alarm the Syndics called in the engineer once more, and on his final report decided to renew the roof and floors (all save the ground floor) in wood. It seems that all preparations for renewing the structure in concrete were 'scrapped,' and that this accounts for the firm stand made by the contractors, who of course did not admit that they were in fault. Much expense had been incurred in consulting experts. In order to settle the question of liability with the architect, the Syndicate agreed to an arbitration, and the architect accepted this. At this stage the issues become very technical in the hands of lawyers, and matters became so serious that the contractors commenced an action at law against the University. To avoid this, it was found necessary to propose a compromise. In other words, the University had to pay for the fault of others. Its representatives, the Syndics, seeking to make the best of a bad job, were drawn by the accident into a false position. Delays and wavering policy, due to the conscientious variations of expert advice, left the contractors a legal advantage. A Grace of the Senate had to be passed empowering the Syndics to make the best terms they could under the advice of the University solicitor. The actual payments made are given in the Accounts, 19 Feb 1881. The result of this affair, foreseen by many, had to be accepted, and in time the voices of grumbling died away.

RELIGIOUS MATTERS

To speak of Cambridge as it was in my early days, and to compare the life then with that into which the lapse of time has brought us, without any reference to religious usages, would be a neglect that no excuse would justify. I must deal with this matter somehow, and I begin by admitting that I may be ill informed as to the facts of the present. I was not in my youth under any serious pressure to take Orders, though I well knew that kind relatives and friends hoped I might take that course. Therefore on quitting School for College I kept an observant eye on religious doings. I was conscious of a queer feeling in relation to College Chapel, a feeling that at first I did not myself understand. At School the attendance had been simply a part of the daily routine. The only question was, how much time you could allow for the morning toilet without being late for Chapel. No choice entered into a plain matter of discipline. College rules were based on a principle superficially the same, essentially different. Of fourteen services in the week you were required to 'keep' six. Failure to do this was punished by gating. But you were free to keep them in the evening, if you thought morning Chapel at 7 a m too early. Also, if you kept two Chapels on Sunday, you could get off with three in the rest of the week. In undergraduate language this was expressed 'two on Sunday count for three': the official version was 'those who keep two on Sunday are excused one in the week,' a refinement which then seemed to me childish. But nobody seemed to expect anything nearer to commonsense from the Dons; and after a brief experience no more did I. I came to see that the old simple notion of discipline was for me at an end, and religious observances henceforth on a new footing. Spiritual influences needed to be very powerful if they were to retain their virtue in the tainted atmosphere of a tariff.

Now, in order to get any spiritual nourishment out of the Chapel services, you had to take it in with you, and in some highly developed form. The mere presence of a number of men who were only there under compulsion was an automatic

check on devotional warmth. Nor could it fairly
be said that the presence of the Dons supplied any
emotional stimulus. Some were known as good
easy-going men, some as bigoted adherents of this
or that ecclesiastical school, some suspected of
general indifference, others were so colourless that
no opinion could be formed about them. John
Mayor was regarded with affection by those who
met him in the course of duty, on the ground of his
vast learning and sympathetic innocence. But the
limitation of his influence may be guessed from a
sermon that I heard him preach in Chapel. No
narrow bigotry marred the flow of his humankind-
ness. He said quite plainly that he hoped in a
future state of bliss to meet Socrates and Epictetus
and other virtuous representatives of the Pagan
world. To a few of us this large-minded utterance
was welcome. To far more, I fear, it rather suggested an unwelcome introduction to 'ancients' of
whom they hoped they had got rid for good, or
would get rid, if and when their examination days
were over. In short, to them the prospect offered
was rather disconcerting. One preacher alone did
in my experience reach the mind of a large part of
the audience. This was Josiah Brown Pearson, a
junior Fellow. He knew that a number of the men
were intending to take Holy Orders, and that some
of these were living in habits unsuited to that
profession, habits that it would be difficult to
discard. And he frankly dreaded the moral effects

of a sudden revolution, however thorough the change might be. I well remember the sensation caused by this discourse. It was printed by request, but what struck me most was the unaffected wonder at his action. Were College Dons going to cease fumbling, and preach to (and at) their Undergraduates? The question was soon answered. Two of the elders took to preaching at each other on issues of orthodoxy. One evening there was even a slight ironical applause from the benches. Sermons in Chapel were for several years dropped altogether. The differences between the chief antagonists were too embittered for even the Master's tact to compose them.

In me, a raw and bewildered youth, the religious usages gradually bred disgust. I was just beginning to be aware that dogmas, fundamental and presumed certain, were being called in question by men of high character, and that clerical replies to their criticisms generally took the form of abuse or personal slander. College Chapel offered no help in my perplexity. I went to some University Sermons, and heard fine discourses, some of them soothing, some animated, but none that really touched the difficulties I had to face. So sometimes on Sundays after evening Chapel I went on to St Edward's Church, where F D Maurice was preaching. It sounded very sweet and noble, but I couldn't make head or tail of it. The well known Omar Khayyam lines [quatrain xxvii] exactly describe my position. The natural effect followed: I found myself in revolt. I had succeeded beyond hope in my Academic course so far. A Fellowship was within reach, unless I should fail in the Tripos. But I saw clearly that I could no longer honestly take the religious Test. Scholarships would come to an end. Money borrowed for my schooling had to be paid off out of my first earnings, and without a Fellowship the prospect of doing this and making a decent living was small. My case was one of a number at that time. The opportune relief afforded by the Act of 1871 has been referred to above. Before I leave this topic, let me say that the religious conditions were not to the best of my belief more unsatisfactory at St John's than elsewhere. In some Colleges they were certainly worse. A system in which all Undergraduates were assumed to be members of the Church of England, and were therefore compelled to frequent its ceremonies as a matter of discipline, was out of date. The serious public did not really believe in it. Levity and evasion were its manifest fruits. In one distinguished College a short service, much favoured, bore the local name of the 'Sunday three-fifteen Express.'

While writing of Chapel matters I am reminded of an episode very interesting to me, which I venture to record as an experience illustrative of a state of things not likely to occur again. In May 1869 the new Chapel of St John's was so far completed as to be ready for the opening ceremony.

A large number of old members of the College, subscribers to the fund raised for defraying part of the cost of the work, attended by invitation, and were entertained at a lunch or early dinner in Hall. The great majority of them were clergymen. Undergraduates and Bachelors were not forgotten, but room for their entertainment had to be found in the Racket courts at that time standing on the southern side of the Cricket field. In this department of the celebrations old and young bore a willing and genial part. On that festival day formality took a secondary place: it is even true that a lady dined in Hall as a guest of the College. She was the daughter of an eminent Banker, and soon after became a Peeress.

The great opening service was held in the new Chapel on the morning of the twelfth of May. An important feature of the proceedings was the sermon, preached by Bishop G A Selwyn, noted for his vigorous episcopate in New Zealand, and then recently appointed to the see of Lichfield. An old University oarsman, accustomed to ride or swim to any scene of duty, he was a formidable person. In the University pulpit I once saw and heard this mighty militant, and I could not help feeling thankful that I was safe in the gallery. Well, he gave the Johnians in Chapel a stirring address, and naturally appealed with force to College sentiment and solidarity on an occasion so momentous and (as was then thought) so triumphant.

But, in referring to the College membership as a whole, his fighting spirit led him to strike an unhappy note, peculiarly out of harmony with the business of the hour. From the range of brotherly love and sympathy, including all absent members, he deliberately excluded the 'recreant' Bishop. For Colenso, whom he thus vainly strove to excommunicate, was also an honoured member of St John's. Such was the bitterness of orthodoxy fifty-six years ago. Yet to our new school of Divines Colenso is already a 'back number.'

I had left the Racket courts and strolled back into College all the better for my dinner, curious to see what was going on in the company of my elders. Entering the Hall, I found them in great decorum, but not of the kind that comes forth by fasting. Good humour beamed from their faces, and the speeches were just beginning. These I wanted to hear, and the gangways were so crowded with extra tables that I saw no way of getting within earshot but by mounting a table and walking along it. This I did, and the genial clergy let me pass on till I was close to the dais. To my alarm I found myself next to the vicar of St Mary's Shrewsbury, who knew me well: but he greeted me with a smile.

Of the speeches in general nothing need be said. But, when the Master rose to propose the health of all absent members, I was witness of a memorable scene. With a tact never excelled even in his own utterances he led his audience through topics fitted to arouse their patriotism and pride. At a well chosen moment he glided into a manly refusal to countenance any exception to the general goodwill on an occasion when unity was the dominant note, the idea underlying the whole. And he wound up by boldly coupling the toast with special mention of the name of Bishop Colenso. Many who heard him must have wondered how the mass of clergy, most of them undoubtedly hostile to Colenso, would take the Master's challenge. But the parsons generously rose and cheered, like the good fellows they really were. I believe I was the only undergraduate present, and the scene made a deep impression on my mind. I came away with a better opinion of my elders.

On that morning, at the regular hour of 7 0, was held the last service in the old Chapel, already half dismantled. It was handed over to the 'builders' for destruction. There are photographs that shew the beautiful early work, belonging to the old St John's Hospital, revealed as the demolition went on. It may be that religion gained something by this great effort of ecclesiastical zeal, but I doubt it. Be this as it may, the exquisite proportions of the First Court are lost for ever by the removal of the oldest portion of it. Cambridge has one less link with the venerable past.

In earlier pages I have recorded the interest I have always taken in religious phenomena, and I can hardly shirk some sort of comment of a general kind on this side of Academic life. The stale and unprofitable Chapel-keeping of my undergraduate days is a thing of the past: compulsion by punishments has long given place to moral pressure, the extent and efficacy of which I have no means of judging. But I think I may safely say that many good and sincere men now take the view that a College Chapel is a rallying-point, a symbol and expression of inner unity among men not professing identical doctrines. About this aspiration there is nothing common or mean. But I wonder how far it attains its end. No doubt the several circumstances of Colleges vary considerably. It is evident that ceremonies are not neglected: sermons and music are more in use than of old. A notable movement is the growth of College Missions working in populous places. This seems to me an indication that the Academic clergy are nowadays less convinced of the innate wickedness of young men. It is thought a good thing to engage their interest in the welfare of others; that is to provide an outlet for philanthropic feelings early in life, feelings which formerly were unsuspected or ignored. So far well. But with this movement goes a tendency to elude dogma, to combine the activities of men holding different doctrinal views. There seems to be a sort of groping towards an agreement that religion is not a creed but a life.

I am not presuming to offer any opinion for or against this movement, but am trying to appraise its significance in the Academic world of today. That it leads to a position flatly contradictory of that dominant since the Council of Nicaea in 325, seems to me quite clear. Philanthropic Christianity is superseding its predecessor Muscular Christianity as an influence urging Man to set about remedying his own ills by his own efforts, and to trust that Brotherhood and Service to fellow men are in themselves offerings acceptable to God. But meanwhile what is doing in high dogmatic circles? Tenets, that well within my memory were essential to orthodoxy, are being threshed and winnowed by restless Divines, apparently in the hope that the grain left for spiritual sustenance will be sufficient when the breeze of criticism has borne the chaff away. Now Man can only use the powers with which he has been endowed. It is idle and dishonest to blame the Cathedral Deans and other theologians who are engaged in disestablishing dogmas: we must not muzzle the ox that treadeth out the corn. But surely there is a point of view to which they might fairly give more attention. There are a few, and those not the basest of their species, who long ago reached much the same conclusions as these Divines are promulgating now. Some of them have had to bear evil imputations undeservedly: most of them have had to pass their lives under some degree of disadvantage. For the world is apt to regard as at least 'unsafe' those on whom the hierarchy is supposed to look askance.

It is to the honour of Cambridge that the University has in recent years shewn itself more tolerant than the world outside. But I would not go so far as to say that such prejudices have even here been of none effect. I do say that, if our theologians are prepared to reshape orthodoxy on a model that will cancel a good deal of constructive heresy, they may as well do so openly and at once.

Thousands of men, serving their several Churches and Connexions, are giving the best years of their lives to work inspired by ideas that are the kernel of Christianity. I find it hard to believe that the best of them, those who took to this life from a simple appetite for doing good to others, would be changed for the worse by discarding the dogmatic equipment that seems to gall so many of their superiors. The ordinary Priest or Minister in harness has neither the leisure nor the learning to follow up theological problems and find solutions. Many have no turn for such subtleties; they take what has been supplied to them, and go about their daily tasks. But nowadays one is hearing on all sides of the difficulty of filling the churches and chapels by any other means than those in use for secular entertainments. Why is this? I answer, what else can you expect, when the busy labourers depend for dogmatic material on leaders who appear to be in grave doubt as to their own meaning? What are the rank and file to do, when men who qualified for high preferment by orthodoxy give public

utterance to views that have stamped other men as
unorthodox? In what other profession would such
conduct pass muster as a mark of professional
loyalty and honour? Must not the driving force
of any organization be enfeebled, when its rules
are explained away and treated as null by its own
members? Now where, if not in the Universities,
is a tonic remedy to be found? If the people need
religion, and religion needs emotion, and emotion
is transitory when lacking sincere conviction, is it
not important to ascertain in the twentieth century
what that conviction really is? How are men to
speak from the heart, if their message is drawn
from doctrines all adrift? Are the forces represented
by George Herbert and Richard Baxter, by Wesley
Simeon and Keble, to be left behind as obsolete,
dying out through the failure of a dogmatic apparatus largely the work of oriental Greeks? Here
is an issue that Academic Divines are in duty
bound to face. That is, unless they are satisfied
that the material benefits of Science are of themselves sufficient to promote the wellbeing of mankind.

I sometimes wonder whether, if I had been
ordained on the clear understanding that I accepted the beliefs of the Church of England, if I
had in due course attained preferment, if I had
then become convinced that fundamental doctrines
were erroneous, I could have kept my place in the
ranks of the Establishment. A hasty negative seems

to me inadmissible. The Divines who remain in office, but explain away their supposed creed, are surely not acting without a reason. In any case they are as good men as those who agree with me, and often better. In the so-called Free Churches the Ministers are more directly dependent on the will of their Connexion, and the question can hardly present itself in the same form. One of the most melancholy figures I ever met was a Minister discarded by his congregation for unorthodox views, and driven to seek secular employment in middle life with a family to maintain. But his religious principles stood the test. In the Establishment, the eighteenth century saw several clergymen resign their posts owing to objections to the Book of Common Prayer. Nowadays it seems the practice to agitate while in office against doctrines that a cleric is supposed to have accepted and to have undertaken to defend. Such is the crude view of ordinary laymen, perhaps superficial; but it accounts for their general indifference and distrust of modern clerical movements as means of upholding 'true religion and virtue.'

An attentive French critic[1] thus describes a typical English parson. 'Le recteur du village, homme du monde, ancien élève d'Oxford, théologien ami de la science, bienveillant pour les philosophes modernes, véritable Anglais qui ne redoute pas les compromis et garde son bénéfice

[1] André Chevrillon, *Études anglaises*, ed 1920 p 283.

sans prendre au pied de la lettre les trente-neuf articles de l'Église établie.' The writer rather admires this figure as an element in the stability and dignity of country life. Now our English capacity for compromise has stood us in good stead, at least in political and social matters. And there appear to be some who fancy that a movement of the same kind will serve their purpose of religious revival. But perhaps the cases are not analogous. In the political and social sphere we act (or seem to act) independently of control and under no obligation to render an account of our actions to a superior power. The very existence of Theology postulates a different position in matters of religion. Theologians may fairly be invited to consider whether a plan of give-and-take will really meet their difficulties. That road may lead to acquiescence but does it lead to conviction? And what are the prospects of a revival carried on by the unconvinced? It is not easy for an observer to answer these questions. Nor is it well for the professionals to avoid them.

BUILDINGS

To describe the buildings that have been set up since my Freshman days, or even to make a bare list of them, would be a wearisome and useless undertaking. Nearly all those belonging to the University would have to be included, and they are their own justification. College enterprises

would also be many, from the big front of Caius
to the new out-building of Clare. All those designed
for Women Students would be in the list. These
growths suggest to me one or two general remarks.
First, the common aim of all is comfort, more
accommodation, more effective use of modern appliances, than was possible in the old buildings,
however skilful their internal modification might
be. In one or two instances there has been some
attempt to make arrangements favourable to simple
and economical habits. But I do not think this can
be regarded as the general character of the movement. The boarding houses at schools compete
with each other in offering higher standards of
comfort to attract pupils, and Colleges are doing
much the same. Again, the respect shewn to the old
buildings varies greatly in different Colleges. In
the desire for more rooms, we see new blocks erected
so tall as to dwarf the fine old courts. Sometimes
a College, under the spell of an ambitious architect,
even pulls down ancient fabrics, beautiful in themselves or necessary parts of a proportional scheme,
and builds instead something quite out of keeping
with its surroundings and in a taste that happily
enjoyed only a transient vogue. Most striking of
all is the obvious fact that haste (often allied with
megalomania) has in some cases brought its own
punishment. Those Colleges that have not been in
a hurry have profited greatly by noting the mistakes
of their neighbours. Whether any new court has

yet been so designed as to make (for instance) central heating easy, I cannot say: but this detail illustrates my remark as to haste. For a building erected in the first half of last century is probably not less refractory to modern adaptations than one of the Tudor period. Naturally, the artistic effect of the new blocks, set up under very various conditions during the past fifty years, varies greatly, and opinions will differ. From this point of view I humbly give my preference to the new building of Magdalene.

While speaking of College buildings, I call to mind a quaint experience I once had during my tenure of office as Junior Bursar of St John's. The outer door, 'sporting door' or 'oak,' is I think still in use as a means of privacy in College rooms. Its actual structure varied a good deal in various cases. Some had a solid frame, with a surface of thin boarding on both sides of the door, leaving a small vacant space between the boards. In order to prevent letters from falling into this space, the slit that served for letter-box had a special lining of wood. Thus a letter could slide through and fall on the other side of the closed door. In course of time the lining might, and sometimes did, get damaged. I have heard several stories of letters found after many years lodged between the two surface boardings of a door. Somewhere in the nineties of last century a certain door had to be repaired. The carpenter found a number of old letters and cards in the between-boards, and they were brought to me. It was only in a few cases necessary to open and read them. Some, addressed to old members long deceased, contained invitations eloquent of the undergraduate hospitalities of a past generation. Among them was one that bore a common name, and it was thought that it might belong to a barrister of the name. Though the postmark shewed it to be some thirty years old, it was sent unopened to him. In his reply repudiating it he suggested that we (the Senior Bursar and I) might like to see it. It was the tract usually sent round in October, exhorting Freshmen to Chastity. I do not know a better illustration of automatic irony in Academic life.

THE BOROUGH

Side by side with these Academic developments there has been an improvement not less remarkable in the Borough. Being still sufferers from the narrowness of many streets, and reminded day by day of the perils of motor traffic, we are apt to forget the efforts of the municipal authority to grapple with problems ever growing in extent and gravity owing to the rapid growth of the town. Two important steps taken within my recollection have led to a concentration of power in the hands of the Borough Council. One was the abolition of the old Improvement Board, an unwieldy and lethargic body of doubtful repute, which allowed things to be done that ought not to have been done. The other was the improvement of relations between the University and Town authorities, which among other advantages has done away with a cause of constant friction. The special duty of maintaining decency and order in the streets no longer rests on Proctors, who had long proved their general unfitness for the work. Now and then an exceptional Proctor did well: too often the office suffered in repute through alternations of slackness and injudicious zeal. Things are much better now. The Proctors deal with members of the University only: members of the University sit on the Borough Council. Some day the Borough Magistrates may find a means of teaching Undergraduates to respect the rights of others in the streets. A money fine has no terrors for owners of motor cars.

Among the material improvements in the Borough none is more notable than the drainage system. In my younger days it was a common undergraduate saying that the Cam was only kept going by the Town sewage. The truth was that a very small percentage of that product ever reached the river. I remember seeing the old brick sewer opened in King's Parade. It was full, up to within less than two inches of the top, of a solid deposit of ages, that was dug out like foul black cheese. Yet with such drains the health-record of Cambridge was not bad, and the opposition to reform only gave

way under Government pressure. Disputes over
many competing schemes occupied many a year.
Interesting facts as to the nature of the ground in
various parts were disclosed by trial-pits and
borings. When at last a plan was adopted and
carried out, the stench from the man-holes of the
new sewers was horrible, and a further outlay for
ventilation was necessary. This was a success, and
the Town is now sweet enough. But the present
generation can have no notion how great the
revolution has been. Not less remarkable is the new
policy of making open spaces contribute to the
public enjoyment and general brightening of the
Town. Parker's Piece is no longer a cheerless waste:
Christ's Pieces, laid out with paths and trees, forms
a much needed meeting-ground, where crowds can
listen to music in the summer months. More remains to be done for the benefit of the new suburbs
between Barnwell and the Hills Road. But this
side is not forgotten, and it is to be hoped that the
making of the new road across the Fen will lead
to a great improvement of the swamp known as
Sheeps Green. In the old town several opportunities
of widening streets have been turned to account,
but the difficulty of doing anything of this kind
on a large scale is extreme, and the College
authorities not always helpful. With the supply of
water gas and electricity by private enterprise the
Borough Council has not yet interfered. Having
no interest in any of these companies, I am free

to say that this abstention seems to me wise. For many years to come the municipality has quite enough to do without undertaking these functions of supply. On the whole, Cambridge has no reason to be ashamed of the working of its Local Government.

So the Town goes its way, enjoying the general good health of which an excellent water-supply is a prime cause, in spite of jerry-built streets in the newer quarters and unredeemed slum-yards in the old. The main fault of the Cambridge people is an easy-going acquiescence, a trustfulness of which scoundrels every now and then take advantage. I need not enlarge upon the fraudulent solicitors who within my memory have from time to time absconded leaving behind them suffering and ruin. Nor need rate-payers be reminded that they have been victims of foul play with the Borough accounts. Such things happen elsewhere, but I doubt whether any town takes them so coolly as we do. Gambling in one form or other is surely at the back of these misdeeds. The cases of College Servants, who forfeit the most permanent of situations through dishonesty, are cruel illustrations of this lurking evil. Happily, they are rare. If it were possible to invent a machine to discover the comparative moral merit of various classes, I fancy that in respect of steady and solid qualities College Servants would be very near the top of the list. But outside their ranks the number of lads exposed to special temptations in an University town is inevitably large. The errand-boy who constantly visits rooms deserted in afternoons, the lodginghouse-keeper's son envious of undergraduate lodgers, the hangers-on who dawdle about places of resort in hope of something turning up, are specimens of the demoralizing influence of which I am speaking. Much more could be said on this topic. To me it seems greatly to the credit of Cambridge youths that on the whole so little mischief comes of it all. Meanwhile we have two forces competing for good and evil—the Boy Scout movement and American films.

I must not forget the change that has taken place in the spirit and conduct of elections in the Borough. Cambridge used to return two Members of Parliament, and in my early years the contests were on the old lines, between Conservatives and Liberals of the types common for many years after the Reform Act of 1832. Even after the Act of 1867 the constituency was small, but wavering in its party allegiance. Old traditions of violence, with a touch of Town-and-Gown fighting, sometimes led to rioting. In the election of November 1868 there was a serious row at the meeting of streets near Christ's College. The town roughs had the upper hand and drove back a number of Undergraduates. Two Johnians were penned against the gate of Christ's, which had been closed for good reason. The College Porter generously opened the wicket and rescued them from the angry mob. As he was shutting it again, a heavy stone struck him on the head and killed him. Looking back from the elections of 1923 and 1924, when a much larger constituency, now returning only one Member, polled in perfect peace, it seems strange that so great a change can have taken place in so short a time. We are often told that you cannot make people moral by Act of Parliament. Very true: but that argument is used to discredit all legislative change. That much good can be effected by legislation is proved by experience, and the Ballot Act of 1872 is a case in point.

RIOTS AND DISCIPLINE

The traditional Town-and-Gown rows belonged to an earlier social condition. Within my memory, nothing but an occasional collision between small parties on the Fifth of November recalled the legendary battles of a past generation, and gave rise to stories, mostly apocryphal. The dying out of barge-traffic on the river gradually put an end to another source of conflicts. Bargees were not in a hurry to clear the way for College boats. Boat captains were not always conciliatory. Hence there was friction, and now and then a fight. Tales of prowess floated in the air. A famous strong man, Haydon of Emmanuel, was said to have picked up a bargee and thrown him into the river. For this I cannot vouch, but anyone who saw him row in the Emmanuel Four would not doubt his ability to do so. The relations of Town and Gown have undergone since those days a marked change, perhaps not wholly for the better. In 1898, when an Honorary Degree of LLD was conferred on Lord Kitchener of Khartoum, there was great excitement. In the evening a huge bonfire was made in the Marketplace. The materials for it were largely got by robbing the timber appliances of works in progress and carrying off rails and palings from fences along the Backs. There was in short wholesale destruction of private property. No proper precautions had been taken for the maintenance of order, and the riotous proceedings went on practically unchecked. But perhaps the most significant part of the affair was the cooperation of Undergraduates with Town roughs. The scene was of course deplored, but too late. Since then I have on one or two occasions noted a tendency to cooperate in minor disorders of the kind. It does not appear that combination for destructive purposes springs from any desire to obliterate the barriers of class. It is nothing more than a passing alliance of two mischievous forces, and a little 'class-consciousness' would be no bad thing. I have known great waste of wood take place at a time when all fuel was scarce and many of our poorer neighbours were finding it no easy matter to keep the home fires burning.

That a host of full-blooded youths will now and then break out into demonstrations that let off steam, is a mere fact. And, so long as they destroy nothing, the relief of monotony may well excuse a little folly. The occasional 'rags' of recent years are harmless enough. We elders are apt to forget our youth, and lose sight of the boredom that our juniors sometimes feel in the round of Academic life. The only serious objection to Mock Funerals and other processional displays seems to be the expense. They certainly do seem to advertise the University as being still a haunt of the rich. Hoaxes have a great attraction for the youthful mind. But they do not admit an early repetition, since they put people on their guard for several years after. Yet the visit of the Shah of Persia many years ago (a Town hoax, I think,) was followed after an interval by a similar visit from Zanzibar. In both cases Municipal dignitaries were victimized. In the former case there was a great reception-scene at the Station, but no Shah, and much heartburning in the Town followed the discovery of the hoax. On the latter occasion an amusing difficulty arose. The undergraduate Zanzibaris were solemnly shewn round places of interest, and expressed their thanks by the mouth of an equally genuine interpreter. But King's Chapel gave them a searching test. They could not put off their turbans for fear of instant detection. To wear them in the Chapel would have spoilt the whole adventure by an act of 'bad form,' and undergraduate opinion must not be outraged. So they had to find a plea for declining admission to a seat of alien worship. The best sort of 'rag' seems to be a midnight raid of one College on another, as when the Caius men made off with the German gun from Jesus Close. Such an exploit exercises vast ingenuity and secret organization, and harms nobody.

Unhappily it is hardly possible to avoid some reference to an outrage of a very different character, in which the danger of contagious excitement, leading Undergraduates to disgraceful action, was painfully exhibited. The question of Degrees for Women agitated the University in the years 1920 and 1921. Partly by accident (the Coal Strike), partly by errors of management, a vote on important proposals, which should have been taken late in June 1921, was deferred to the middle of October. Thus it fell in a time when the student population was resident in full force. During the May Term the opposition had made great play with protests from Undergraduates. These were 'unsolicited' or 'spontaneous': in short, not openly invited. The cry of 'a Man's University' was enough to evoke them. The word went round that to admit Women as Members of the University would mean the decline of manly qualities, and the failure of Cambridge in athletic competitions. Against such a result hundreds of innocent youths signed a protest, determined as they were to vindicate our preeminence in sports. At that time things were going well for Cambridge in this department, and the prospect of continued victories over an effeminated Oxford was alluring. By October the elder students had many of them gone down, and the Freshmen had come up, as usual, nothing if not 'manly.' It was that time of the year when undergraduate emotion is normally most unstable. When the vote of the Senate, unfavourable to the Women, was declared, a mob of students thronged the approach to the Senate House. A Member of the Senate told them of the result amid cheers, and actually suggested to them a visit to Newnham. I was on my way home in that direction. Shortly after passing the bridge by Queens' I became conscious of a dull sound growing nearer and clearer. It soon explained itself. A solid column of Undergraduates came along at a double, and the beat of their footfall was impressive. It was easy to guess their object. I guessed their number at about 1500 (the local paper made the same estimate), but my only remark was 'not many King's men in that lot, I think.' So they went on their way to the blind and brutal outrage at the Newnham Gate, which needs no description.

That what was done was actually done by a few, perhaps a very few, can hardly be denied. But it is also true that a great impulse to violence was furnished by the presence of a mob. Ringleaders feel that their satellites expect them to do something, and excitement promotes a mischievous rivalry. What the mass thought of their leaders,

I cannot tell. But from a point of vantage I watched them as they began to move away from the scene in driblets, and I was struck by their quiet and subdued bearing. Many were no doubt at heart decent lads, lured into the adventure as a joke, and quickly passing from amusement to disgust. The next morning found the Academic world in a stir of shame and repudiation. Leading Undergraduates, headed by the Stroke of the University Boat, expressed their indignation and contempt. A fund was subscribed for making good the material damages, which were of course for the moment overestimated. Sincere apologies and profound regrets were tendered and gracefully accepted. In short, the student world did what it could to redeem itself from the disgrace brought upon it by unworthy members: young blood recoiled from passive acceptance of shame. The Town looked on in amazement at the doings of 'the Gentlemen,' in which it had borne no part. The London papers commented on the affair, for which even those opposed to Women's Degrees could find no excuse. Meanwhile the more bitter of Graduate opponents, while repudiating all responsibility, were not above ridiculing the overestimates of material damage. An interesting sequel brought Academic proceedings to a close. The Graduate who had egged on the student mob to their attack on Newnham was solemnly charged by the Proctors before the Court of *Sex Viri* with contravening the Ordinances of the

University. He pleaded guilty and expressed his deep regret, and was severely reprimanded by the Vice-Chancellor. That the reprimand was well deserved, few will deny. I presume that this official gesture was at least partly meant to free the Senate from all suspicion of sympathy with the offender's act or readiness to condone it. But the name and description of the culprit were officially withheld. It may appear unseemly to find fault with the generous use of mercy shewn to a wretched creature. But the fact remains that this concealment left the Senate collectively and individually under a certain stain. Unofficially the name of the guilty member soon leaked out: indeed it was known to many from the first, and particulars of his record were accessible in *Crockford*.

The whole episode was one at which Cambridge men may well blush. Why then revive an unwholesome memory? Because the evil exposed is not really on the surface, not a mere effect of temporary aberration on the part of old or young, in short of human frailty common to us all. It has its roots deep in the conditions of Academic life. If you venture to hint that the disciplinary system of the University is ineffective, you are generally met with the reply 'What can you do with such numbers? In moments of keen excitement a few Proctors (be they ever so good) are of no avail.' Now the real gist of this is that disciplinary control depends in the last resort on moral force. We have no need to be ashamed of this. It is when we inquire from what quarters and by what policy the needful moral force can be brought to bear that we begin to feel uneasy. At intervals of a few years 'regrettable incidents' occur. These we deplore, lament, etc etc. Some blame the Proctors, who are very seldom in fault. Some detect a lowering of the social standards of Undergraduates, and so on. But no serious effort is made to diagnose our own shortcomings or to devise a remedy. What is the underlying cause of this impotent lethargy? I find it in the solemn and timid acquiescence in the lack of unity which is a grave defect in our Academic constitution. Nothing effective can be done by the University for the preservation of order without the hearty cooperation of the Colleges, and there is no central authority powerful enough to secure this without hesitation or question. The discussion of Regulations governing the use of Motor Vehicles (*Reporter* 17 Feb 1925) seems to illustrate this point. Vice-Chancellors and Proctors come and go in due cycle. Colleges are jealous of their 'autonomy,' and the votes of College staffs are weighty in the ordinary course of business before the Senate. So they are left undisturbed in an atmosphere of mutual forbearance. When some untoward event arouses general indignation, this or that College punishes one or more of its men as it sees reason to do; another College, not less concerned in the matter, may do nothing. Yet there is a manifest opening for effective College action of a simple kind. It is not the 'Blues,' the heroes of the student world, that are the ringleaders in enterprises of a discreditable or destructive character. They have a position, a dignity to maintain. And undergraduate sentiment is normally sound on questions of 'good form.' Even Freshmen, the majority of whom have been lately associated with the cause of order in their several schools, are only likely to act badly under bad leading. Now I say boldly that College officials, knowing more about their men than outsiders can know, are the right persons to mobilize student opinion against excesses such as no indulgent criticism can justify. But, until effective pressure can be put upon these virtuous gentlemen to act as under a common responsibility, I fear nothing will be done. As individuals they are in touch with the students to a degree undreamt-of fifty years ago. And I believe that Undergraduates in general are a better lot than they were in my time.

In short, I hold that the real hindrance to improvement in the means of wholesome discipline and putting an end to the scandals referred to above, lies in the wrongly valued 'autonomy' of Colleges. Each waits for others to begin, and there is no power to give them a start. At the back of this is the demure timidity of Residents. Men undeniably able and well disposed seem to shrink from saying or doing anything that may not commend itself to their friends and acquaintance whom they must often be meeting. The way in which they hang back and catch at every pretext for hesitation is an unhappy phenomenon. When any important issue calls for settlement, an appeal to Non-residents at once reveals a striking contrast. Non-residents, generally satisfied as to the excellence of their own Academic generation, are not prone to hesitate on the supposition that a change from the conditions of that golden age may be for the better. The majority are automatically indisposed to change, and arguments for it do not go far with them. What is needed to move them is a 'cry' of some sort: and this throws decisive power into the hands of the Resident clique who furnish it. The never-failing negative is thus a constant menace, enfeebling the will of Residents, and increasing their timidity. Under the present constitution, by which voting in person is required, and not a quarter of the Senate can vote, this negative pressure is exercised by a majority of a small minority. I know of no institution in any country the government of which has to be carried on under such a palsying condition as this. It is a case of capricious action unattended by consciousness of responsibility.

REFORM AND REPRESENTATION

It is to be hoped that the reforms to be introduced by the Executive Commission will go far towards making an end of this situation. The report

205

of the earlier Royal Commission no doubt hampers them in various ways, and may lead to changes that are far from wise. For instance, there is an underlying assumption that all men are qualified to do research work, and that you have only to put pressure on them all to secure notable results. Experience will perhaps not fulfil this hope; but evidently the risk is to be taken, whatever inconveniences it may involve. But as to the position of the Senate it seems that the Commission has a free hand. The present absurd system can hardly be allowed to continue, and the awkwardness of having two bodies, Senate and Parliamentary electorate, side by side is not likely to be ignored. A further question appears behind,—the relation of Academic bodies to the national Representative system. What is the general characteristic of such bodies that renders their members deserving of a second vote? The fundamental principle of Representation can only be reconciled with 'fancy franchises' if and when these exceptional privileges are attached to special qualities by the marked expression of which the whole community is likely to be benefited. Now, what does a Graduate body, acting as a constituency, offer in justification of its 'fancy franchise'? In Great Britain at least, such bodies are as a rule noted for adhesion to the past and dislike of change. If a check on hasty reforms is desirable, here is an element highly qualified for bearing a part in political action of a 'suspensory' character. For in the power of seeing objections to whatever is proposed the truly Academic mind is unrivalled. Cambridge, already thronged with beknighted individuals, might prove the nursery of potential Peers, not inferior to some of recent creation, and frankly political. How would this affect Conservatism? Not much. The good old rule, of opposing everything until you are ready to take the credit of doing it yourself, is not to be annulled by a mere structural change. Deep-rooted in human nature, it is a main fact of politics. To this it is owing that Conservatism plays an effective part as practical agent of political changes.

Long observation of the Graduate as Voter has not made clear to me his marked superiority to the Man in the Street. That is, so long as his function is to decide whether A or B shall be a Member of Parliament. If we had by Referendum to vote for or against proposed measures, the higher average of mental training might perhaps justify a preferential claim. But here comes in the practical consideration that, while preferences are always more or less invidious, the total number of votes concerned is insignificant. There is a risk that this total may be held an adequate concession to whatever superiority Graduate judgment may possess. And in counting heads it amounts to very little. Now, while a nation remains at all politically sound on a 'self-governing' basis, suspensory checks on legislative haste operate best by the way of moral force. And this influence the Graduates, if they are what their admirers portray them, are able (and perhaps willing) to supply. Indeed not a few of them are doing so at this very moment. Therefore I doubt the wisdom of the present arrangement, and hold that by our 'fancy franchise' we are paying too dear for the privilege of returning Members to the House of Commons. Times are changed since University Seats were almost as useful to a Government as the control of pocket Boroughs.

THE GREAT WAR

The war of 1914–18 and its sequel, the greatest and most awful event within my memory,—how can I sketch its effect on Cambridge in a few short paragraphs? But I must say something. Thoughtful observers had for years noted the drift towards some great upheaval. Governments had for their own convenience so acted as to blind the nation's eyes to the danger. We were unprepared both materially and mentally, and Cambridge had its share of well-meaning folks unable or unwilling to look facts in the face. Yet of alarming facts duly recorded in the newspapers there was no lack. For my part, recent visits to Germany had left on my mind a general impression of the change in German manners. What we call 'swollen head' had under Prussian influence taken the place of the old-fashioned *Gemüthlichkeit* formerly characteristic of most Germans. The insolent bearing of the military was at its height, and afforded a significant commentary on the various items that were now and then cautiously recorded in our Press. So during the famous twelve days of suspense I never doubted that Germany meant to have war. On Sunday the 2nd August H F Russell-Smith, junior Fellow of St John's, a young History student of high promise and personal charm, called to invite my signature to a memorial from a number of Graduates, urging the Government to keep this country out of the impending war. I replied that war was inevitable, that the intentions of Berlin were manifest, and therefore I could not sign anything to weaken the hands of our Government. It was sad, terribly sad, to have to say No to such a man in such a cause, but as an older student I felt myself better able to judge the situation than this noble youth, and I refused his request with gloomy forebodings. He was one of the victims of the war.

A number of Residents, some of them apparently well qualified to judge, signed the memorial. But by the 4th August we were at war, and a dark shadow lay upon us all. In Cambridge men of military age at once made ready for army service, either as privates or as officers. While this was going on, and the already equipped Divisions were being sent abroad, five sites for camps were being prepared round the town for other troops hurriedly mobilized to receive final training—two for infantry, and one each for artillery engineers and a Welsh ambulance corps. Of the last unit I saw a great deal, as their exercise-ground was on Caius cricket-field, and the Colonel was billeted on us. I need not detail the visits my wife and I made to other camps, seeking like our neighbours to do what we could for the men. But I cannot avoid recording the horrid evidence of unpreparedness that struck one everywhere. For instance, the infantry encamped on Midsummer Common were taken for long marches in the hot weather. I have seen them coming back with the sweat streaming off them. Getting into condition, no doubt: but what they wanted was to take off their shirts, wash them in the river, and then dry them. But there were no spare shirts, so they could not do this. If the weather had turned wet, I believe the tents would have become hospitals. Many local people came forward with shirts etc, but the need could not be fully met, and the poor fellows doing what washing they could in the Cam by Jesus Sluice were a pitiful sight. I heard of volunteers sent to a lonely spot on the Essex coast to camp in a swamp without even a rifle per man, and other conditions to match. Such was the state of things at the outbreak of a great war.

Weeks and months went by. The various units were gradually fitted for the front and withdrawn, generally at night. Early in 1915 the camps were deserted, and the last of the old Regulars gone abroad. Meanwhile Cambridge was selected as the place for a military hospital. Wooden sheds, at first on a small scale, were erected in haste. In order to give the wounded plenty of fresh air, these were open in front. But the patients suffered so much from cold and wet, and the nurses from chilblains, that the later wards had to be built more snugly. Local doctors served in khaki, and were borne on the army strength: some went off to service abroad or in other hospitals at home: none were idle. So far the formation of Kitchener's new army proceeded by voluntary enlistment, and town and county rose well to the call. But the past policy of Governments, dissembling the approach of danger, caused many to hold back. To some the navy seemed enough guarantee for our security. The notion that we must support foreigners in order to save our own freedom was to many a shock, an incredible novelty: they could not go back on old beliefs all in a moment. They were not Conscientious Objectors (though such persons were not unknown), but simply waited to be fetched. I need not describe the steps by which compulsory service was finally reached in December and Great Britain stood to arms.

The sudden fall in the number of students, and the departure of many of the younger Graduates for military or official duty, left the University gloomy and lame. Women students and Orientals were still about as usual. Girton and Newnham staffs, with other ladies, were 'doing their bit' as opportunity offered: a convalescent hospital close to my house was worked under a Newnham Don. Some scientific departments did war-work for the Government, and everybody was looking to see how he could by his own effort set free younger men for public service. And whatever was done was done in a depressing atmosphere of rumours, a situation most trying to the more thoughtful and better-informed people, on whom the duty of keeping their neighbours cheerful inevitably rested. In the early months of the war, when the great delusion of a Russian army passing through England to France was at an end, there were disquieting reports of disasters concealed for fear of alarming the public; and these not only at sea, for the damage to some towns by airship raids was kept as dark as possible. The danger from submarines was brought home to all by the strict rules for the distribution of food. The patient rows of people waiting their turn at the Food office were a striking feature of Cambridge life under the strain of war. In the town streets and in the villages a common sight was the card placed in the window, notifying the absence of some member of the family at the front. The awful sufferings of men in the trenches during the hard winter of 1914–5 were not concealed, and news of deaths was sent to relatives with wise promptitude. So things dragged on somehow until the first corner was turned, the Government was roused to frantic energy, and the war passed into the stage of an organized conflict of science and resources.

One feature of life in Cambridge will not easily be forgotten by those who were in residence during the war. Airship raids were a constant menace, and the eastern counties were specially exposed to them. Norfolk in particular lay right in their track, and Dereham suffered severe bombing. The local objective was probably the Norwich military centre, but some of the machines flew much nearer to Cambridge, and the danger to King's Chapel was obvious and alarming. It was necessary to discontinue the lighting of all towns, for without this precaution any place might at any time be bombed during the dark hours. So Cambridge was wrapped in a medieval gloom for some three years, and men had to grope their way about the streets as best they could. Special constables patrolled the several parts of the borough and enforced obedience to the official order. And we escaped the fate kindly designed for us in Berlin. But it was a doleful setting in which we lived, ever receiving doleful news. Yet only once did I hear a voice of despair and a suggestion that it was high time to make peace on any procurable terms: and this came from a man of the purest patriotism, who was 'doing his bit' to the best of his power.

I need not follow up the events of the later years, which were developments of the earlier hurried efforts. University and Colleges were just kept going by makeshift arrangements. Offices were combined or kept vacant. The old men did their best to fill gaps. The Union was kept in active being by extra donations, and was found useful as a club-room for the military. Cadets in training for commissions soon became an important element of the University population, and the Colleges were convenient places of residence. Hastily trained, one batch after another was sent off to the front. Such was the grim reminder of the wastage of war. These things are a solemn and dreadful memory. They brought some old residents into touch with the whole British Empire, for many of the cadets were Colonials. At the end of the war came the picturesque invasion of officers in the USA army, a very fine lot of fellows, who billeted themselves in College rooms and threw themselves into Cambridge life with characteristic energy. One of them rowed in an LMBC boat and carried back to America his oar, the record of nightly bumps. Meanwhile as the scattered members of the University dribbled back to Cambridge, survivors of the exodus, they began to confer with each other. Like many up and down the country, they were deeply impressed with the conviction that there had been too much idle drifting and apathy in the period before the war. They were young, and not disposed to sit down tamely and acquiesce in a mere resumption of former aims and former ways. So they met in a body, discussed apparent defects in the Academic systém, and chose sub-committees to draft proposals for changes desirable in the interests of efficiency. These proposals were eventually printed as a sort of unofficial report. The signatories are I believe now generally known as the 'Underforties.'

This movement was carried on without inviting public notice; in fact so privately that as a 'back number' over 40 I only heard of it by accident. I had an opportunity of reading the manifesto, but could not get a copy for myself, and can only give my impressions of its contents. With most of it I found myself in sympathy, but some of its detailed suggestions seemed trivial, and others betrayed a lack of experience. And some of the signatures appended to certain proposals afforded ground for legitimate surprise. An older man might wonder whether the authors had a clear notion of the effects, direct and indirect, that this or that action was likely to produce. But on the whole it was a manly and well-meant scheme. If some of its articles implied too severe a censure of the past, this seemed to me excusable in the circumstances of the moment. Several years have now gone by, and various indications have led me to doubt whether all the 'Under-forty' were (or still are) earnest reformers. Time has done its work, and I fancy it would not be easy to reunite that company now on the footing of a common policy. Be that as it may, their undertaking was surely not an idle waste of energy. There is however no harm in protesting that among the elder men are to be found steady supporters of onward movement in the University, and that even the youngest of those who signed the manifesto in question is by now probably well aware of the fact. The fine old man who died a few weeks ago [26 Dec 1924] was a notable specimen.

In due course the ending of military war led to the designing and erection of War-Memorials. The main object was simple, to record the names of the fallen, in appropriate surroundings. Naturally the details of execution have been very different in different cases. The University shares with the County and Borough the fine monument set up on the way to the Station. The Colleges went their several ways. King's have not neglected or misused their exceptional opportunity: they have a memorial not to be surpassed in its quiet and dignified repose. Jesus too have done well. Of the others, very various in design and position, I would only refer to that in the chapel of Trinity Hall. A general tablet on the chapel wall is supplemented by a complete register of names (with details of corps and rank) inscribed in a vellum book. This book is lodged in a little recess in the panelling of the ante-chapel, easily consulted, and giving more particulars than could be conveniently cut on a wall. It is not only an exceptionally full record, but interesting as containing some names

of men who fell in the service of the enemy—
Austrian or German gentry who had in earlier
years been members of the Hall. I admire this
Memorial, original and free from ostentation,
breathing silent sorrow, and (pardon the fancy)
seeming to suggest that what their men once did
their successors would at need do again. This is a
fit and solemn honour to the memory of their dead.

LOOKING AHEAD

And now here we are, launched for good or ill
on a career of struggles to 'make good' after a
convulsion that has rent the world, and has left
us face to face with problems brought into evidence
by the recent strain. With these the younger generation will have to deal. An old man can only contribute remarks based on a long, but perhaps mis-
taken, observation of Academic politics. It has long
been clear that, if the University is to respond
cheerfully to the call of national needs, the Senate
must either be able to express its will by a majority
or suffer a restriction of its powers. A thorough
consideration of possibilities will probably end in
the adoption of the second alternative in some form
or other. The practice recently followed in more
than one case, of offering to the Senate two con-
trasted proposals on the same subject, and leaving it
to reject the one and confirm the other, is notable.
As a method of legislation it seems ill suited to

the operations of a large body that never polls 25 % of its numbers, very seldom more than 5 %, and indeed seldom divides at all. And there are usages, arising from certain mental prepossessions, that in our resident life often lead to undue waste of time and result in disappointment. One is the plan of forming a half-and-half Syndicate to propose a means of dealing with some highly controversial matter. Now and then this is done, in the hope that stalwart opposites equally balanced will hammer out an acceptable compromise. This plan may succeed when one or two of the body are not so stalwart as was supposed: otherwise a tiresome deadlock is apt to ensue. Not wholly unconnected with this topic is the prevalent delusion that an indifferent chairman is a sort of guarantee that all varieties of opinion shall have an equal chance of a fair hearing, and that a wise decision is likely thus to be attained. This is a mistake, springing from the confusion of indifference with impartiality. Indifference in the chair nearly always results in weakness of control, and the final decision of the body is at the mercy of one or two pushing members clever at seizing the advantage of a passing moment. Meeting follows meeting, and the members present on two successive occasions are perhaps not exactly the same. The indirect reopening of issues already settled protracts the wearisome debate, and in the end the majority are out-manoeuvred by the im-

portunate few. But a strong chairman with views
of his own is urged by his sense of honour to see
that all sides get a fair chance: and I do not believe
that our society is unable to produce such men,
impartial but firm, able to promote an orderly
relevance, and to judge when to use a casting-vote
and when to abstain.

University business is nowadays so extensive and
so complex—with every prospect of becoming
more so—that the above remarks, however mis-
guided they may be, are at least not irrelevant.
Whatever we may think of the changes now approaching, we all wish that they may be so worked
in practice as to secure the highest efficiency in the
coming age.

One internal issue that seems to me important
and in the long run unavoidable is the relation
of Colleges to the University as a whole. Commissions, inquisitive or executive, seem never to
grapple with this question boldly. It is now proposed to give the University not only a power of
taxing the Colleges but a right to insist on part
of the College Fellowships being reserved for endowment of University posts. Meanwhile Colleges
are to keep 'autonomy' as before. That this arrangement may lead to complications in the
practical working, seems to me not doubtful, and
I am tempted to wonder why the risk is ignored.
Autonomy exercised under the pressure of public
opinion has worked well; but it has done so in the

hands of corporate bodies homogeneous in character, not subject to capricious disturbance by the operation of external rules. It looks as if these bodies might become less homogeneous under the new dispensation, and less fitted to carry on steadily and wisely the functions they have now discharged fairly well for many years. I hope I am not idly dreaming when I suggest that it might be better to tax them somewhat more and interfere with them less. I seem to see ahead a choice of alternatives; either to do as I have just suggested, or to bring the Colleges under a central control as residential departments of a residential University. In the latter case the governing bodies of the Colleges would be appointed by the University. This sounds too doctrinaire a scheme, allowing too little for slow development guided by experience. It may be so. But at present there seems on the other hand an excessive tendency to forget that Universities and Colleges are the outcome of deliberate acts, charters and so forth, the details of which are (and must be) revised to meet the change of needs. That the College system has, under external pressure, become a valuable asset of national education, nobody would deny. Whether it would not gain by the competition of an extended and more vigorous Non-Collegiate organization is perhaps a fair question. With emoluments pulling Collegewards all the time, the Non-Collegiate body has justified its establishment under grave disadvantages. From its birth in 1869 it has quietly thriven in the same period as has witnessed the internal and external revival of the College system. I cannot help thinking that, in the great variety of human circumstances and needs, further development of this institution would be a good thing. But without some improvement in its financial position it can hardly have a fair chance of displaying its possibilities. I cannot forget that within my own memory several of the most useful and eminent characters in Church and State have been men who had not been to a fashionable School or an University. Therefore, when it is argued that a practical monopoly works well, I cannot grant the implied conclusion that an effective rivalry would not work better. Students vary greatly in character and in their family traditions and circumstances, and I cannot see what the University stands to lose by offering every opportunity to suit the convenience of all varieties.

Not wholly unconnected with this question is one that has often occurred to me in past years as I watched the course of events. Why are the Heads of Colleges regarded as a Body the members of which have some common attributes, however different they may personally be; while the Professors are treated as Units, and it seems that no distinctly Professorial opinion on any subject is regarded as a possible fact? Yet Professors are University officials, while Heads are only College officials, whom the University neither appoints nor pays. Professors of full title (not to count Readers and University Lecturers) are now 57 or more. Heads are still 17, as they have been for now more than a hundred years. No doubt the present situation is a survival from the time when not only were the Colleges the University, but the several Heads, each in his own Society, were in a position of vastly greater responsibility and power. And it is kept in being by the fact that the Headships provide the succession of Vice-Chancellors, and thus serve to defer for a time the consideration of a difficult problem in a very busy period. So an arrangement by which five, or at least four, seats on the Council of the Senate are reserved for an Order of 17 Heads, passes without effective challenge; and the direction of business is largely left in the hands of men who are assumed to enjoy the necessary leisure. The Professorial Order has four seats also: but their position is different. The active head of a great teaching department can hardly give himself up to the endless variety of business details, nor would it be well that he should do so. It seems not un-likely that a time will come when Professors will not care to shoulder this burden in person. If in such circumstances the expression of Professorial opinion on the Council is still felt necessary, may it not become desirable that the Professoriate should elect representatives, instead of appearing in person?

As I have on an earlier page referred to the

attraction exercised on me in my school days by masters who came from Oxford, I feel bound to say something of what I may call the Cambridge Model. That there is a certain quality imposed on many, perhaps a majority, of our men by the subtle influences of tradition and surroundings, long observation forbids me to deny. But it certainly does not affect all, at least in such a degree as to produce a marked and easily recognizable type. If that be the most desirable result, I think it is more successfully attained elsewhere. So long as I can remember, we have never lacked a due proportion of Cranks, often highly estimable men. A cause probably not unconnected with this effect I seem to discern in the extreme subdivision and segregation of studies which has more and more prevailed here, resting on the basis of old tradition. What looks like innovation is often no more than a fresh application of principles now (1924) about a hundred years old. When the Classical Tripos was founded (1824), it was and long remained the rule that it carried no Degree with Honours: that was only granted through the Mathematical Tripos. To confine the latter to Mathematics only, to liberate the former from a restriction that had become galling, to establish Triposes for Moral and Natural Sciences, were steps on the road leading to separate recognition of all studies on an equal footing. And it is the simple truth that as an active purveyor of learning the advance of Cambridge from 1824 to 1924 has been prodigious. That general mental cultivation as an equipment for later life has quite kept pace with this special development, is not to be affirmed so confidently. Not long ago the head of the Medical School for urgent reasons challenged the University to provide some guarantee for the better education of Science students, whom he grieved to find unable to express themselves in decent English. Hence the now universal requirement of what are called 'essays.' I hope this measure has extinguished illiteracy: anyhow I am thankful not to have to read them. I fancy that the defect crying for remedy is partly due to the prevalent use of slang to economize thought; partly to the fact that 'students' work harder than they did fifty years ago—that is, at their own subjects. They have less leisure for other intellectual interests; though, if I am not grossly misjudging them, their intellectual average is higher than that of their predecessors. Under the conditions of modern pressure, a general Entrance Examination with firm insistence on a good standard seems the most desirable and practical solution. That Cambridge has been famed as the University of great men is a fact that we are not prone to forget. But we do not with equal candour hold the truth that several of our greatest owed little or nothing to the official nurture of their day. Whether, when the new system is in full swing, and every student gets the benefit of expert direction and supervisory control, we shall be more or less renowned as a cradle of mighty nurslings, who can guess?

I ask to be forgiven if I venture to comment on one branch of study in particular, of which I really know nothing. Cambridge has long been the chosen home of high Mathematics, and we all regard this fact as our glory. No name stands in our record more honoured than that of Newton, and his successors have not suffered the torch to grow dim. Sixty years ago perhaps the majority of Fellows of Colleges were men elected on the score of Mathematical Honours; at all events they formed the strongest element in that class. Now one of the things I most clearly remember noticing in my younger days was the marked tendency of such men to conservatism of the most rigid and fruitless type. To any idea of movement, any recognition of the duty of adapting Cambridge to the necessities of a changing world, they were inaccessible—I do not say blind. Their influence and votes were an important part of the opposition to reform of which I have spoken above. I remember what a shock it was to me when I found that men who had been high Wranglers in their time could and did simply refuse to take account of the serious questions that were arising before their eyes. I had and have an almost superstitious reverence for Mathematicians, and this phenomenon puzzled me. Things are now changed, and the resident Mathematicians are a much smaller percentage of the whole body than they once were. Yet even now what I may call the mathematical view of things is sometimes curiously in evidence, and I am not alone in detecting it. Some (more than of old, I think,) escape it through having other interests of a humanizing kind. These are one of our finest Academic types. But others seem unable to avoid the mental bias that is easily created by a habit of calculation in which all units are assumed to be equal if not identical. In political problems past or present, this attitude is apt to be misleading. Human beings, and the conditions in which they live, vary immensely, and in thinking of them and their welfare this consideration needs to be ever kept in mind. For instance, your Mathematician is well aware that the abstract 'economic man' never existed in the flesh, and probably never will. But, when the question is one of how best to act for the good of the average man, it will not do to argue on the supposition that all your units are equal. In Academic life there sometimes occurs a difficulty arising from the terms of a deed of foundation, enjoining preference to a candidate possessing some particular qualification, when two or more are otherwise equal. The phrase *ceteris paribus* is classic in this connexion. On this Dr Bateson Master of St John's remarked 'but the *cetera* never are *paria*.' Dr Thompson Master of Trinity said 'how much poverty is equivalent to a false concord?' No, political or Academic, all matters concerned with men (and women) need the application of considerations in which the variety of individuals is taken into account in framing rules and laws for general use: and no function of legislation is more delicate than this.

FAREWELL WORDS

In setting down on paper these recollections and experiences of an obscure life, over the course of which I have had little or no control, I venture to incur the reproach of triviality. It was possible to offer no such record; it may be that silence would have been best. I am well aware that nobody who may read these pages is likely to feel any desire to lead the sort of life I have had to lead. But I am not writing to win recruits for a party or a cause; I am only recording the main facts that have come under my observation and the impressions made on the observer. I have imposed on myself no small restraint in the way of anecdotes. If I once began telling true stories of strange individuals merely for the fun of the thing, goodness knows when I should stop. Cambridge life in particular affords a vast fund of material, and has been to me an unfailing source of amusement for more than fifty years. On our little stage there is room for manifold developments of human character, mostly harmless, and men freely act their parts with earnest and natural ease. I suppose the younger generation do not differ from their predecessors much in this respect. The social crudity of a bachelor regime has passed away with the coming of female influence, but I think it is still true that unrehearsed effects of personality amuse a thoughtful spectator more genially and instructively than laborious efforts of professional entertainers.

To set down naught in malice is a good rule, and I have tried to follow it. Nor is it hard for one who is at heart an Optimist. Frankly, I do not believe that we are a degenerate people: I do believe that, if we do not solve the grave population-question without delay, we may become degenerate. The warnings of Eugenic enthusiasts cannot be neglected with impunity. It is true that reformers are apt to be hasty, and to make insufficient allowance for the time and sustained effort needed to achieve subtle reforms without the setbacks of violent and wasteful revolution. But it is in Universities that the best opportunities exist of testing theories and gradually supplying a stimulus to public opinion and practice. And that Cambridge will bear a notable part in this region of public service I do not doubt. What interests me in the doings of this great University is above all things the splendid onward movement which it has been my privilege to witness in the course of some two generations. The forces underlying this movement are surely not spent. Cambridge will rise to her duty as she has risen in the past. Mistakes will now and then be

made as heretofore: but some one, now a junior
Graduate, will look back upon her progress, as
I do now, with pardonable pride. He may feel,
as I now feel, the itch of fore-reaching curiosity
as to what the sequel of his own time shall be. But
he too will have, I fear, to do without foreknow-
ledge, passing from the Academic scene with the
prayer *Floreat Cantabrigia.*

ENVOI

Whither, oh whither, asks my eager soul:
   To prophecy she makes no vain pretence:
dark are the coming years that onward roll.
      I mark the what and whence,

The rise and fall of hopes in earlier days,
   The clouds that lowered and the suns that shone,
The griefs and joys that made me blame and praise,
      watching the world move on.

And, ere I part, to you I give my blessing
   who, in your turn for strenuous action free,
along the paths of duty boldly pressing
      shall mould the age to be.

With single-hearted zest and calm endeavour,
   yet not unmindful of an honoured past,
build on as though ye meant to build for ever;
      so may the fabric last.

March onward, free from doubt and hesitation:
   We elders vanish, ousted by the new:
but in their course a coming generation
      will do the same by you.

APPENDIX—READING PARTIES

Intimate experience of undergraduate life in vacation away from Cambridge, never shared by many, seems now to be a faint tradition of the past. Clough's poem stands to Reading Parties as *Tom Brown* does to old-time School life. The age is one of Museums and Laboratories; but the Literary departments are almost as much affected as the Scientific, owing to the extended use of fixed plant in Libraries and Museums. In the old days of the Classical School it was possible to get serious work done in temporary quarters among non-academic surroundings. For ten Long Vacations I spent two summer months with pupils away in distant places, generally without anything to mar the joyous freedom of happy common life. Of course the first essential was to get together a congenial company. This was not as a rule difficult, for one lively and popular man attracted others and made recruiting superfluous. The chief detail of organization was the formation of a cooperative library. At a meeting in the May Term I read out a list of books and recorded the name of the man undertaking to bring this or that book for common use: each had his own private list as well. This plan worked: I do not recall a single case of default. Nor did I expect it, knowing that undergraduates are habitually loyal and responsive to trust. Finance was simple. A fixed sum was to be paid by each to my account, and this too never failed. I transferred the total to a local bank and made all payments. At the end of our time I produced a balance-sheet and paid back to each member an equal share of the remaining surplus. This seemed to give satisfaction.

For myself this Reading-party enterprise was not, and was not meant to be, financially profitable. In the earlier years I did as other 'coaches' did, setting and revising exercises and generally making actual teaching my business. But I became convinced that of teaching such as was then in vogue it was easy for a student to have too much. With more reading, under the sympathetic direction and help of an elder student sharing their common life, the men developed more healthily and were less liable to 'go stale.' So in the later years I more and more dropped formal teaching and fees, till they practically ceased altogether. I turned my own time to account by doing work for College lectures in the coming year, and was thus able to keep up a certain freshness, though my discourses lacked erudition. On the whole these summers were not only good for health of body: in the close study of characters, and in gaining thorough acquaintance with interesting neighbourhoods, I learnt much that I am glad not to have missed. In particular the unreserved contact with juniors of various types helped me later as a College Tutor to understand the undergraduate view of things, and this for many years, till the lamp flickered and went out. But I must not dissemble the truth that responsibility for youths away from home and College was now and then a sore burden; all the more as we were always quartered by water, salt or fresh, and even the best swimmer may misjudge currents or overestimate his powers. Add the risks of faulty watermanship or careless rock-climbing; think of parents in the background, excusably liable to uncharitable judgment of a leader under whom a disaster should occur. I am thankful that the bad moments were few. They were only on occasions when I was temporarily out of sight and young blood was tempted to do what was for good reason forbidden. So long as one was on the spot (in the boat etc) there was no undue anxiety, as any risk was the same for all. And a reasonable discipline was treated as a matter of course, as it is by normal undergraduates. In all departments where official control by elders does not operate they soon set up rulers of their own—and obey them.

In 1871 we were a small party at Bray on the Thames, and combined steady work with enjoyable rowing and bathing in weather mostly fine. A trip to Eton gave me another peep at the scene of my rejection in 1862. I remember walking one day out to a village where the Stocks then stood in good repair on the green. Some of us learnt the art of poling the old-fashioned clumsy punts then still in use on the river. An old photograph records us as a group, seven in all, one of whom was W P Brooke of King's, afterwards father of Rupert Brooke the poet. It was at Bray that I discovered the high qualities of this interesting pupil, who fully justified my estimate of him. The kind attentions of the Vicar and his family are not forgotten by me. In Bray Church I first heard a sermon in which Darwin's views on Evolution were calmly treated as a fact not inconsistent with Christian doctrine.

In 1872 I had temporary School work at Shrewsbury, acting as deputy for my old master John Rigg in charge of his Form (the Shell) and house (Rigg's Hall) till his death. For so young a man this was no small responsibility, and I felt some pride at getting through it and (as several things proved) with success. In the house ample instructions made my course clear, and the experience was not wasted. The Form had suffered from being taken by deputies who only stayed for a few days each, and it needed to be taken firmly in hand. It was no easy task to hear the lessons of over 40 boys, usually taken in two divisions, keeping one set in order while the other was being heard. But the boys soon responded to the genuine interest I found in them, and the Shell was noted for the rarity of punishments. Some changes in the routine work were plainly welcomed, and at the end of Term in July we parted on my side at least with regret. The later careers of some of my boys have been an honour to themselves and their School. Mr Moss had only been there as Headmaster since 1866, and was struggling with difficulties of which I learnt something. Whatever his weak points, he had at all events the great merit of not worrying Assistants who did their duty efficiently. This, as I learnt later, was not the practice of all Heads.

In January 1873 I became a College Lecturer at St John's, and gave up coaching on a considerable scale. In the summer the first of nine successive reading parties (6 pupils) was at Coniston. My friend E B Moser had ridden over from Kendal and found quarters for us. We worked hard, and the rainy season did not stop hard exercise. What with the Fells and the Lake we were kept in good condition. Two of our team were fishermen. I fear they poached a little at first on private becks, but the kind courtesy of Mr Marshall of Tarn Hause winked at the offence and gave them leave to fish in any of his waters. I had a Rob Roy canoe, in which I navigated the lake, rough or smooth, with joy. Our party was a very happy one, though I noted only five fine days in eight weeks.

The Long of 1874 was spent at Port Erin, Isle of Man, a charming spot with a bright little blue-water bay and the bold mass of Bradda Head on the north side of it. At that time the place was not much 'developed,' and therefore unreservedly enjoyable. Steady work and good bathing and boating kept us (6 pupils) lively, and expeditions on foot and a cricket match at King William's College gave variety. Fish, chiefly mackerel, were easily caught in the tide-run off Bradda from a small boat, but a larger craft, kindly lent us, had to be laid aside. She was so leaky that we had hard work to bring her and ourselves safe back into port. There was much of interest in the country round and some of us were glad to get a notion of the ways and institutions of the island. The railway to Port Erin was opened during our stay, a doubtful improvement from our point of view. With the Vicar and Curate of Kirk Christ Rushen we were on the best of terms, and liked the people generally. One little episode sticks in my memory. Two of our party were out dining at the chief country house near. The other five were suddenly called from their evening meal by a lady in wild alarm, who told us that one of a family lodging on the cliff front was drowning. In gasps she revealed that it was the beautiful Miss T. The five arose and hastened to the scene. I found the best path and got to the beach first. The girl had already been pulled out, and had not really been in much danger. I was just in time to stop her being hastily drenched with brandy. We had only to offer our arms and conduct the mother and two daughters up the cliff path, while the other two men went off to find a doctor. I took the recovered daughter, dripping like a sea-goddess in her bathing robe. Behind me came our best swimmer with the elder lady, short of breath and gasping 'oh what a different procession it might have been!' Next day a gentleman called on us to thank us for our help, but (such is life) gave the credit to one of our number who had not

234

been present. That this little affair gave vast pleasure to us all, need hardly be said. The undergraduate welcomes an unacademic experience. And that the women selected the comeliest of the party to receive their thanks, facts notwithstanding, was an amusing proof that they had not omitted to keep an eye on their neighbours.

The summer of 1875 found a party of 9 pupils and two coaches (for H Cowie shared the work with me) at Fishguard in north Pembrokeshire. This turned out to be an ideal place for our purpose. What was then called the Great Western Hotel served for our headquarters: some of us lodged close by. The contract for our feeding was performed liberally, and saved much trouble. Dr Wathen and his family welcomed us most kindly, and so did Mr Rowlands the Vicar,—indeed everybody. The country, lovely and in all ways interesting, offered various attractions, and long tramps were never wearisome. Fishguard Bay was for boating or bathing a resource that seemed designed for the delight of such a company as we were. Many miles from the railway, the place was unspoiled, and Goodwick, now the harbour terminus of the GWR, was just a few houses on a hillside. It had its little halo of tradition. Close by was the spot where the last landing of an enemy had taken place, and that not a century before. The story of the ignominious surrender of the gang of French ruffians is amusingly told in Fenton's *Pembrokeshire*. Mr Rowlands told me that when he first came to Fishguard an old inhabitant who remembered the affair gave him this additional information. The actual landing was an insane venture, the cliff being only scaled with great difficulty. This I verified from a boat. The true explanation of it was that the French were conducted to the spot by a Welshman, a prisoner in France, who belonged to that part of the county. In order to effect his own escape, he pretended to be an ardent republican eager to serve France, and offered to guide an expedition that would set Britain in a blaze. Put in charge of a gang of undesirables, he took them to his own neighbourhood, slipped away at the first opportunity, and left the wretches to their fate in the rough peninsula of Pen Caer. True or not, I fancy that the cause assigned by Fenton had something to do with their speedy collapse. A ship laden with wine had lately been wrecked on that coast, and the invaders, after eating all the food they could find, got helplessly drunk on the liquor ready to hand in all the local houses. Hence there was time for the Yeomanry to appear in force and win a bloodless victory. A story in which, as Fenton remarks, 'the finger of Heaven was manifestly visible.' So much for the doings of 1797. I return from this digression to more peaceful scenes.

In the middle seventies there was a religious revival, connected with the Moody and Sankey mission from America, going on in several Cambridge Colleges. St John's was one of those affected by it, and my comely pupil above referred to was one of the apostles. He was bent on doing something for the benefit of Fishguard, and asked the Vicar's leave to hold a service on Sundays in the School. Mr Rowlands granted it (what he thought of it privately I never knew) and of course I could not openly make objection, though I agreed with the rest of the party in disliking the proposal. It seemed in questionable taste for a student youth, a mere stranger, to pose as missionary in a place swarming with Christian ministers of many sects, before even ascertaining that the present religious activities were a failure. However, preach he did, and found not a few hearers. He even delivered a farewell sermon at the end of our stay, to the disgust of our happy and virtuous company. After this experience I always stipulated that preaching should be no part of reading-party functions.

The ecclesiastical arrangements of the neighbourhood were of interest to several of our number. Under the vigorous rule of Bishop Thirlwall most of the little parish churches had been rebuilt within recent years, but parsonages were in some cases still lacking, and the incumbents living in Fishguard. One of these, an exceptional old rogue, was a notorious character. Rumour told of him that he had secured his benefice by some queer practice years ago, and had been guilty of base frauds on trustful people since then. It was said that the old Bishop had tried to get rid of him, and failed. In conversation with him I gathered that he did not suffer from any self-reproach, and that he was in fact a pillar of the Church ministrant. He had a great contempt for what he called the 'low Welsh,' being himself really a degraded Jew. So he long existed in peace and disrepute, to the discomfort of other clergy. The position of the local clergy was not a very easy one. Long neglect in the past had promoted Dissent, clerical incomes were small, and a bitter Sabbatarianism was sometimes in evidence. Cambridge had a little prejudice to overcome. When the coming of our party was announced, Fishguard opinion had been divided. Some thought that a gang of clerics were on the war path, bent on tiresome interference with local usages; in short, ecclesiastics of priggish temper, who would frown on local shortcomings. Others expected a band of young 'bloods,' whose doings would shock even the very tolerant propriety of

Fishguard. The orderly merriment of a few lively undergraduates was a revelation to both sections. When we left, we were entreated to come again, and the name of Cambridge stood high. Among the Fishguard worthies with whom we were brought in contact was Albert Furlong, who kept horses and traps, on principles too generous for his own interest. Some years before, he had earned the Humane Society's medal for a gallant rescue at the wreck of a coasting vessel.

I have dwelt upon Fishguard in 1875, because the venture was so signally successful in most favourable surroundings. But eight of the party took their Degrees in 1876, and the recruits for that summer were not as well-matched a band as those of 1875. And the place, Pwllheli in Carnarvonshire, was not a happy choice. It did not offer first-rate opportunities of amusement and exercise either on land or sea. Nor were the people so eager to welcome us as at Fishguard. Our quarters were just tolerable. The landlord, a rigid Calvinist, drank a good deal of rum between Chapels, and was a Sabbatarian of an unacceptable type. It was he who answered my complaint about defective drains with the retort 'trainss! there are no trainss!' This utterance was reported in Cambridge next Term, and someone sent it, in a garbled form, to *Punch*. But this matter was no joke to me, for a low fever was almost epidemic in the town, and deaths frequent. One local youth played in a cricket match against us, and within a fortnight was dead and buried. There were funerals from the houses on each side of our lodgings. It was a blessing that the only one of our party that caught the fever was myself, and I rallied quickly under Dr Hughes. An interesting event was the great Calvinistic Methodist meeting, held that year at

Pwllheli. In a large open-air enclosure the sectarian crowd stood listening open-mouthed to long and resonant sermons—eight in a day, some said,—inflaming their religious passions with Cymric eloquence. By sun-down they were somewhat weary. The medical man enlightened me as to the normal effect of reaction from this excitement. I have no doubt that Pwllheli is nowadays healthier and altogether a more desirable place of resort than it was in 1876.

In 1877 with a smaller but more effective party I went back to the old quarters at Fishguard. In spite of rather bad weather, all went well. I recall no particular experiences of interest. But the merits of the place from our point of view were more impressive than ever.

So in 1878 I returned again, and with a larger company, some of whom were skilled watermen. A local railway had now come within about ten miles, and an attempt was made to promote a passenger traffic by running a coach to its terminus at the slate quarry under Mynydd Preselley, the chief hill of Pembrokeshire. But the venture did not pay, nor was it of much use to us. Haverfordwest was still the real railway base, destined only to be superseded when later the new line to Goodwick was made by the Great Western in connexion with the construction of a deep-water harbour in Fishguard Bay. With fair weather this summer was a great success; one could not wish better. We lived most happily, did plenty of work, and generally throve. I have visited Fishguard twice since, and witnessed the changes proceeding. It is rather melancholy to see the life-centre of the place being transferred to Goodwick, while old Fishguard looks as if it wanted a coat of paint. In 1919 I found the old pier, built years ago to shelter the little creek that served as the local harbour, already in sad need of repair, and a general air of depression down by the quay-side. But even in decay the old place was charming. I know no better station for a party of vigorous youths of various tastes in a Long Vacation.

In the hard winter of 1878 I set out to explore possibilities at the mouth of Milford Haven. Icicles (a rare sight in those parts) were fringing most of the shores. From Old Milford I went with knapsack to Dale, crossing Sandy Haven in a ferry boat. The old Charon had once been in our navy, and had served in the Federal blockade fleet during the American Civil War. He gave spicy reminiscences of the high pay then to be had, and of the care taken, by means of temptations, that the money should not be brought back across the Atlantic. Dale was a lone cheerless hamlet, but quarters were to be had for a fairly large company, if only I could get the use of an empty house as part of the accommodation. This I managed to secure, and eventually made a bargain for other rooms and for cooking. The kind lady of Dale Castle helped me to a settlement, and I embarked on a venture the rashness of which now amazes me in old age. I had seven good men coming, and all must be ready for them by a given day, and this in a place at the world's end, with no shops, and nothing but the village produce available. So I had to do the catering under difficulties. I ordered a large consignment of groceries etc from London, to be delivered at Haverfordwest by a fixed date, and set out for Dale myself a week in advance. Enough furniture for fitting up some rooms in the empty house was got from Haverfordwest. With help I made them habitable as camping quarters, cleared a way through the tangled growth of bushes in the garden, and walked off to meet the party at the station and to pick up the goods from London. Alas, a clerk at the Stores had blundered, the cases were not come, and I had to suffer grave commissariat troubles and reasonable grumblings for a week or more; also to make a second lonely expedition to fetch the cases.

My 1879 men behaved nobly, and things soon settled down into a groove. But I must confess that I erred in choosing a place with too little country round it open for expeditions. One depended too much on the water, and the wet summer of that year made this trying to men in need of elbow-room. Yet they never reproached me with an error that they could not ignore, and some at least did good work. Good bathing was easily had from Wathick beach. Boating at its best was good, but having to cross the Haven mouth was a hindrance to voyaging in a small boat with a southerly wind. However, we were afloat a good deal. We got supplies from Milford by water, and the usual mid-Long picnic was taken in the form of a most successful voyage up to Pembroke Castle under sail and a hearty row home. I had some anxious times this summer, undeservedly. Bathing at a notoriously dangerous spot, or under conditions known to imply a needless risk, are ventures tempting to warm youths, even when a breach of promise is involved. I found it hard to forgive the offence. But by good luck I was spared the cruel duty of reporting the loss of sons to fathers and mothers.

Not being yet tired of these summer outings, I arranged for a party at Fowey in Cornwall, where I took a house for two months in 1880, engaged a cook and housemaid, and did all the catering myself. Six pupils and I thus formed a household.

With good weather, charming country, and delicious sea, we had a most pleasant time among the kindly Cornish folk. Our rambles took us as far as Polperro on the East and the Carglaze mine (China clay) on the West. The estuary led us up to Lostwithiel and Lerrin, and some of our marketing was done by water. Fowey was then beginning to attract old-fashioned coasters, looking in for cargoes of china clay: for the artificial harbour at Par was silting up and becoming useless. The railway direct from Lostwithiel has since been completed and has opened up the ancient port of Fowey to advantage. Save for a great sorrow that befell one of our number, we enjoyed ourselves thoroughly at Fowey. Even the service on the whole worked well. Only once did the cook give way to drink, when I found her with widespread limbs stretched out on the floor like a star-fish; but the excellent housemaid did not let us go without our dinner. I should note that the supply of fish was regular and cheap, brought over every morning in a cart from Polperro. For a shilling I could then buy a large dish, ample for us all. As at Fishguard, we found some interesting characters, mostly good. Celebrated by 'Q,' Fowey needs no further remarks from me. Life was easy-going there in those days. When we were leaving, the railway people forgot their promise to send for our luggage. An indescribable scuffle was the result. But they coolly met the situation by telegraphing to delay the main-line train at Par, while they stifled our protests by putting back the hands of the Station clock. As we steamed out, doubtless they grinned and remarked 'us was too many for they.'

The year 1881 took me back to the North, where I secured a large house in Keswick and had eleven men with me. Catering for a party of 12 was no sinecure, but our landlady managed to cook what I provided. The weather wept and smiled as it usually does in the Lakeland. But, while there was good walking to be done, Derwentwater was no substitute for the salt sea. Moreover we were a very mixed lot of various gifts and tastes, and never quite coalesced into a temporary social unit, which is the making of a successful party. Considering all things, we did very well on the whole, and some of our number fill a place in my memory. Among the survivors (for seven are dead) is a distinguished Professor. One died in the service of the Delhi Mission. Others have done good work in Church and State. A difficulty that I noted now more than in former years was that men addicted to Games rather than Sports found Keswick somewhat tiresome; and young blood resents anything like boredom. And I was now myself nearly 34, and the difference of ages was beginning to tell. So when we broke up I made up my mind that I had now presented my last balance-sheet and paid my last dividend. As for direct coaching, it had for years been getting less and less. At Keswick I did hardly any, only searching one or two doubtful cases to see that they were safe to pass muster in the Tripos. I just covered my own expenses, and that was all.

So ended ten years of happy non-academic summers, the experiences of which were of use to me in my ten years as a College Tutor from 1883 to 1893. Many a time did I find the benefit of this close association with my juniors when the need of understanding undergraduates was urgent. Perhaps I am unduly optimistic, but my deliberate opinion is that our young men, in all their infinite variety, are a right good lot, taken as a whole. To rule them is easy, once they are convinced that their rulers really care for them. I remember many instances of unhappy official management, by which mere acts of folly were made causes of ill feeling. The old type of Dons were sometimes provocative. Men ignorant of mankind (not to mention womankind) were pushed by seniority into offices for which they were unfit. And personal virtues proved to be no safeguard against unpopularity and contempt. Of moral influence such men could have none. Clumsiness was one of their main defects, and it mattered little whether they erred on the side of slackness or ill-timed zeal. I am happy in the belief that the new generation of Dons are better equipped and wiser than the old. But even now it sometimes occurs to me that a judicious use of the help that could be got from leading undergraduates might be no bad thing. Young men with a good standing among their fellows are not likely to lose their heads and miss the difference between light-hearted folly and vulgar mischief. In an institution devoted to the development of character as well as the distribution of learning, such as Cambridge is, academic discipline is wholesome and effective in proportion as it rests on moral force.

For EU product safety concerns, contact us at Calle de José Abascal, 56–1°,
28003 Madrid, Spain or eugpsr@cambridge.org.

www.ingramcontent.com/pod-product-compliance
Ingram Content Group UK Ltd.
Pitfield, Milton Keynes, MK11 3LW, UK
UKHW020319140625
459647UK00018B/1933